How to Make $800 Per Month Starting Tonight!

A "no-hype" realistic plan you can implement immediately, without spending a dime of your own!

Gerry Marrs

Gerry Marrs Publications

HOW TO MAKE $800 PER MONTH STARTING TONIGHT:
A NO-HYPE REALISTIC PLAN YOU CAN IMPLEMENT IMMEDIATELY
WITHOUT SPENDING A DIME OF YOUR OWN
Fourth Edition (June 2023)

Library of Congress Control Numbers:
HG179 — Personal Finance
HF5386 — Success in Business

Written by Gerry Marrs

Contents

Chapter One

Introducing the Plan

Are you looking for a way to make money from home using your computer? If so, then you're in the right place! In this book, I will show you how to make $800 per month by taking advantage of opportunities available online. I'll provide a no-hype realistic plan that can be implemented immediately and without spending any of your own money. You'll learn how to identify marketable skills, create an effective Fiverr profile, craft high-quality gigs that sell and more. We'll also cover managing client relationships, scaling up and expanding the business, overcoming challenges and staying motivated as well as financial management and long-term goals.

Prepare yourself for a transformative journey that will empower you to take control of your life. Too often, we find ourselves enslaved by our jobs, possessions, debts, and anyone seeking a share of our hard-earned resources. But what if I told you that you can have it all and still have an abundance to share? Imagine indulging in your dream vacation while an automated money-making system works for you, allowing you to spend precious time with your loved ones.

Adopting this money-making method is no small task. It requires dedication and a willingness to make a few sacrifices. Additionally, it's essential to remain open-minded and seek advice from others to become the ultimate money-making machine.

You may be curious about the plan solely based on the title. Perhaps you picked up this book because you're looking for quick ways to earn extra money or seeking a part-time income. In either case, you've made the right choice. I've personally read and purchased around 200 books on wealth, money-making, entrepreneurship, and various other topics that often seemed too good to be true. In reality, the majority of them were just hype, fiction, or outright scams.

I, like many others, have a regular 9-to-5 job, but I desired more. I wanted the freedom to take vacations, pay off bills, provide for my children, and achieve financial security without resorting to a second job. Then, quite accidentally, I stumbled upon a passive income opportunity through writing and publishing my books. I now have several published books and earn a decent part-time income from royalties. However, I discovered a second money-making avenue that requires no investment and can be started immediately. This book will guide you through getting started on this new venture.

By purchasing this book, you're taking a leap of faith. While we may not personally know each other, I feel honored that you trust me to provide valuable information that genuinely helps you make money, devoid of any hype. I take this responsibility seriously. I assure you that after reading this book, you can begin making money almost instantly. However, I must warn you that earning this money will require effort. It's not labor-intensive and only demands a few minutes each day. It's the easiest money I've ever made in my life.

Today presents a remarkable opportunity for individuals to share their ideas, knowledge, and imagination while converting them into a steady income stream using the latest technology and a vast market audience. This money-making plan is so simple that you can dedicate a few morning hours to it, even in your pajamas. You can continue in the afternoon after returning home for lunch, and work on it a bit more before bedtime. The more you do, the more you'll earn. It's as straightforward as that.

You have the power to determine how much money you want to make. You are in complete control of your destiny and, most importantly, your creativity.

This two-part money-making plan is incredibly creative. It allows you to engage your mind, but if you prefer hands-on work, there are opportunities for that too. It's an incredibly flexible method that opens up a world of possibilities once you get started.

I hope this book helps you achieve your goals. While I can't guarantee you'll become immensely wealthy through this method, some individuals have earned enough to buy their own homes. I don't want to hype things up or create sensationalism, but you can generate a substantial part-time income by implementing this business.

The Gig Economy: A New Frontier for Workers and the Modern Economy

In recent years, the gig economy has emerged as a powerful force that is reshaping the traditional work environment. With its promise of flexibility and freedom, this new way of working is attracting a diverse range of people, from students to retirees to stay-at-home parents. As technology continues to evolve at an unprecedented pace, it is enabling the gig economy to expand in ways unimaginable just a decade ago. This article delves into the intricacies of gig work, examining its impact on the workforce and the potential consequences for the modern economy.

What is the Gig Economy?

At its core, the gig economy refers to a labor market characterized by the prevalence of short-term contracts or freelance work, as opposed to permanent jobs. It encompasses a wide variety of industries and roles, from ride-sharing drivers to freelance writers to on-demand dog walkers. Gig work differs significantly from a traditional 9-5 job, as it enables individuals to choose when, where, and how they work, often without the constraints of a fixed schedule or office space.

Who is Turning to Gig Work?

The gig economy is attracting a diverse range of individuals, each with their own unique motivations for seeking this type of work arrangement. For students, gig work offers a flexible way to earn money while balancing the demands of their education. Retirees may turn to gig work as a way to supplement their retirement income, while staying engaged and active in the workforce. Stay-at-home parents can benefit from the ability to work around their family's schedule, providing additional financial support without sacrificing precious time with their children.

Advantages and Disadvantages of Gig Work

There are several advantages to participating in the gig economy, most notably the flexibility and freedom it affords. Gig workers can often set their own hours, allowing them to prioritize other commitments, such as family or education. Additionally, many gig workers have the opportunity to work remotely, eliminating the need for a daily commute and providing greater control over their work environment.

However, there are also disadvantages to gig work. Income can be inconsistent and unpredictable, as it often depends on factors such as demand for services or the availability of projects. Gig workers may also lack the benefits and protections typically provided to traditional employees, such as health insurance, paid time off, and retirement plans. Furthermore, the absence of a long-term employment contract can result in a sense of job insecurity for some gig workers.

Impact on the Workforce and the Modern Economy

The growth of the gig economy has significant implications for the workforce and the modern economy. As more individuals turn to gig work, traditional employment models may be disrupted, leading to a shift in the types of jobs that are available and the skills required to succeed in the labor market.

The gig economy also raises important questions about worker rights and protections. As gig workers are often classified as independent contractors rather than employees, they may not have access to the same benefits and legal protections as traditional workers. This has led to debates over how to ensure fair treatment for gig workers, with some arguing for changes in labor laws or the creation of new regulatory frameworks.

Technology has played a crucial role in enabling the expansion of the gig economy. Platforms such as Uber, Airbnb, and Upwork have made it easier than ever for individuals to connect with potential clients and customers, facilitating the growth of freelance and gig work opportunities. Advances in communication tools and cloud-based services have also made it possible for gig workers to collaborate with clients and colleagues from virtually anywhere in the world.

As technology continues to evolve, the gig economy will likely continue to grow and adapt, presenting both opportunities and challenges for workers and the modern economy. By understanding the intricacies of gig work and its potential impact, we can better prepare for the changes it may bring and ensure a fair and equitable future for all.

In conclusion, the gig economy presents a new frontier for workers and the modern economy. Its rapid growth, driven by technological advancements, offers both opportunities and challenges for individuals and businesses alike. As we continue to navigate this evolving landscape, it is essential to understand the complexities of gig work and its implications for the workforce and the economy as a whole.

Thriving in the Gig Economy: Common Ways to Earn a Living and Navigate the New World of Work

The gig economy has revolutionized the way people earn a living, offering flexibility, autonomy, and greater control over one's work-life balance. This shift from traditional employment models has opened up new opportunities for individuals seeking alternative income sources or more freedom in their professional lives. In this article, we'll explore the benefits of the gig economy and highlight some of the most popular platforms for finding gigs in various industries. We'll also discuss the skills successful gig workers possess and touch on potential drawbacks and mitigation strategies.

Benefits of the Gig Economy

The gig economy has transformed the way people work, offering several key benefits that appeal to a wide range of individuals. Among these benefits are:

- Flexibility: Gig work allows individuals to set their own schedules, making it easier to balance personal commitments and priorities.

- Autonomy: Gig workers often have greater control over the projects they take on, allowing them to focus on tasks that align with their interests and skills.

- Diverse opportunities: The gig economy encompasses a wide variety of industries and roles, providing ample opportunities for individuals to explore different career paths or supplement their income.

Popular Platforms for Gig Work

The gig economy has grown exponentially, offering flexible opportunities for individuals to monetize their skills and services. Among the numerous platforms available, three stand out for their scale, versatility, and offerings—Upwork, TaskRabbit, and Fiverr. Each caters to distinct niches and provides value to both freelancers and clients through dedicated features, tools, and updates. Here's an in-depth look at what makes these platforms indispensable for gig workers today.

Upwork

Upwork remains one of the most prominent freelancing platforms, connecting professionals across the globe with businesses seeking expertise. Its massive scale is evident, with over 851,000 active clients and a gross services volume of $4.14 billion annually as of 2025. Whether you're a graphic designer, developer, writer, or digital marketer, Upwork provides a vast pool of opportunities through its wide-ranging job categories.

Freelancers on Upwork create professional profiles showcasing their skills, certifications, and client reviews, allowing them to build credibility. Clients post detailed project briefs, and freelancers can bid by submitting proposals, outlining their expertise, approach, and pricing. Upwork's robust interface includes tools like built-in communication features, time trackers, and milestone-based payments to facilitate seamless collaboration.

A standout feature of Upwork is its marketplace take rate structure, which ensures fair payment as freelancers gain experience with long-term clients. Additionally, Upwork has ramped up support for remote work, reflecting the evolving nature of employment post-pandemic. The platform also provides enterprise solutions for large-scale projects, making it a go-to for businesses seeking a blend of scalability and skilled freelancers.

TaskRabbit

For those offering hands-on services and local expertise, TaskRabbit has carved a unique niche in the gig economy. By focusing on connecting gig workers with everyday tasks such as furniture assembly, home repairs, cleaning, and moving, TaskRabbit is an ideal choice for individuals looking to earn income by performing tangible, location-specific jobs.

TaskRabbit has introduced several exciting updates, making 2024 and 2025 important years for platform evolution. The updated task categorization system simplifies how Taskers are matched with clients, allowing users to focus more on the jobs they enjoy. The platform also partnered with Robinhood to offer retirement IRAs, highlighting its commitment to fostering financial growth for gig workers.

TaskRabbit's automated cancellation fee feature ensures that Taskers are compensated fairly for client no-shows, which reduces revenue losses and solidifies trust between workers and the platform. Additionally, its partnerships with brands like IKEA and Homary have increased access to assembly and home improvement tasks. These changes demonstrate TaskRabbit's commitment to providing Taskers with both financial security and a growing array of opportunities.

Taskers set their rates and availability while offering their services primarily within their local areas. This model empowers gig workers to control their schedules while fulfilling immediate client needs, fostering a sense of community and trust.

Fiverr

Fiverr continues to be a top choice for freelancers offering creative and digital services. Known for its "gig" system, Fiverr allows freelancers to explicitly define their offerings, pricing, and turnaround times on customizable listings. From logo design to social media management, video editing to voiceovers, the platform attracts clients across industries seeking quick and professional results.

Fiverr stands apart with its intuitive and expansive features. Freelancers enjoy tools for enhancing gig visibility, such as adding portfolio samples, detailed gig descriptions, and client reviews. The platform also recently expanded its categories, keeping pace with emerging markets like AI, blockchain, and digital product development. Its tiered seller levels—ranging from New Seller to Top Rated—help freelancers build reputation and access greater opportunities as they climb the ranks.

Additionally, Fiverr is adapting to the demand for video-based sales presentations. Sellers can now add a video introduction to their profile or gig listings, giving prospective clients a personal glimpse into their skills and approach. With the growing preference for multimedia content, this feature strengthens client-freelancer connections.

For freelancers with specialized knowledge in niche markets, Fiverr Pro continues to provide a premium experience. This segment of the platform allows highly skilled professionals to charge competitive rates while ensuring that the quality expectations for Pro gigs remain high.

Why These Platforms Remain Relevant Today

The continued relevance of Upwork, TaskRabbit, and Fiverr stems from their ability to innovate and adapt to the changing demands of freelancers and clients. Upwork's scalability and integration of enterprise-level solutions make it appealing for long-term project work and remote professionals. TaskRabbit's focus on local, task-based services ensures its appeal in dynamic, community-based markets. Meanwhile, Fiverr's flexibility, creative focus, and advanced features cater to a growing global audience seeking digital services.

These platforms highlight the diversity of the gig workforce, each offering distinct paths to success. Upwork is ideal for professionals seeking structured remote projects; TaskRabbit appeals to hands-on gig workers focusing on local service-based jobs, and Fiverr empowers creative freelancers to market niche skills through bespoke listings.

For gig workers in 2025, the choice of platform depends largely on individual preferences, expertise, and goals. By leveraging the tools and unique features provided by these platforms, freelancers can maximize their earnings, expand their client base, and turn gig work into a sustainable and prosperous career path.

Skills for Success in the Gig Economy

Successful gig workers often possess a unique set of skills that enable them to thrive in this new world of work. Some of these skills include:

Adaptability: The ability to quickly learn new tasks and adapt to changing demands is crucial for gig workers, as it allows them to take on diverse projects and seize opportunities as they arise.

Self-discipline: Gig work often requires individuals to manage their own schedules and deadlines, making self-discipline essential for staying on track and maintaining productivity.

Communication: Strong communication skills are vital for building relationships with clients, collaborating with team members, and effectively conveying one's expertise and value.

Mastering the Gig Economy: Unlock Your Earning Potential with Fiverr

In today's rapidly evolving job market, the gig economy has emerged as a powerful force that is transforming the way people earn a living. With the rise of platforms like Upwork, TaskRabbit, and Fiverr, individuals now have the opportunity to leverage their skills and passions to create a flexible, fulfilling, and financially rewarding career. This book will guide you through the ins and outs of making money through the gig economy, with a special focus on these three popular platforms.

What This Book Will Cover

This book offers a step-by-step guide to succeeding on Fiverr, providing practical advice, proven strategies, and real-world examples to help you navigate this new world of work. Whether you're a seasoned freelancer looking to expand your reach or a newcomer seeking a flexible and rewarding career, this book will equip you with the knowledge and tools you need to thrive in the gig economy.

By the time you finish reading "How to Make $800 Per Month Starting Tonight!," you'll have a clear understanding of how to leverage your skills on Upwork, TaskRabbit, and Fiverr, build a loyal client base, and create a sustainable and profitable career in the gig economy. Don't miss out on the opportunity to unlock your earning potential and take control of your future.

Chapter Two

Identifying Marketable Skills

The gig economy has opened up numerous opportunities for freelancers to showcase their skills and earn a living working on projects they are passionate about. One of the most popular platforms for freelancers is Fiverr, which connects talented individuals with clients looking for specific services. In this article, we will guide you through assessing your current skill set, exploring new skills to acquire, and creating a killer Fiverr profile that attracts clients and helps you succeed on the platform.

Evaluating Your Current Skills and Marketability on Fiverr

Before immersing yourself in the Fiverr platform, it's crucial to assess your existing skills and evaluate your marketability. Consider the following steps:

List your skills: Enumerate the skills you currently possess, encompassing both hard skills (e.g., graphic design, programming) and soft skills (e.g., communication, problem-solving).

Assess your expertise: Determine your proficiency level in each skill, considering factors like education, experience, and tangible achievements.

Research the market: Explore Fiverr to identify popular and sought-after services related to your skill set. This research will help you gauge the competition and discover potential niches where you can distinguish yourself.

Identify your unique selling points: Determine the qualities that differentiate you from other freelancers with similar skills. This could be your distinct approach, specialized knowledge, or exceptional customer service.

Exploring Your Skills and Monetizing Them

To kickstart your earnings through this strategy, you'll need to provide an online-based service. This business attracts individuals from diverse backgrounds, countries, skills, and experience levels. While it's a straightforward process, it's crucial to offer a valuable service that aligns with your strengths and can be delivered relatively quickly. This approach ensures repeat business and multiple opportunities on a nightly basis.

Transforming Your Talents into Financial Success

We all possess a wide range of skills that we excel in. To achieve your goals, you must identify what you're willing to do. Let's begin by considering your background. Have you ever written anything for public consumption? If so, you could excel at editing works of new authors for a fee. If you have experience with computers, particularly in graphic design, you might consider offering your services in creating book covers. With this plan, there are numerous possibilities, and you may find yourself able to offer multiple services.

Analyzing Your Offered Services

Take a moment to step back and reflect on your areas of expertise. Are you skilled in writing? You don't necessarily need a college degree to be a good writer; some individuals write from the heart and achieve remarkable results. Would you be interested in writing reviews for people? Reviews are in high demand nowadays, and authors and new businesses require positive reviews to gain visibility among the public.

Here are some highly recommended talents that can generate significant revenue within this business:

1. Writing reviews
2. Graphic art design
3. Proofreading
4. Editing papers, articles, books
5. Researching topics
6. Painting pictures
7. Singing short songs
8. Performing voice-over work
9. Creating company logos

Making custom videos for people

The remarkable aspect of this business opportunity is that you don't need to be an expert in any particular field. Even possessing a slight talent in any of these areas allows you to start earning money tonight. This is not mere hype; it's the truth, and you will witness just how easy it is in the upcoming chapters.

Let's examine some of these talents and determine whether you believe you can generate income by offering them.

Utilizing Your Intellectual Abilities

Contemporary internet businesses heavily rely on reviews to stay ahead of their competitors. However, many people are reluctant to leave reviews after purchasing a product, which poses a challenge for business owners striving for success. This is where you come in. By receiving free products and providing simple reviews, you can assist business owners while encountering interesting individuals. Best of all, you won't even have to advertise your services, as it's all taken care of for you.

Graphic art design demands a special touch, and many individuals excel in this field. However, numerous people lack the time to create visually appealing designs. If you possess computer art skills and expertise in graphic programs, you can help individuals with tasks like designing business logos, book covers, music CD covers, and more.

New authors, enthusiastic about their work, often overlook proofreading their own material, resulting in the publication of books with unchecked errors. This compromises their credibility. Here, you can offer your editing services, providing constructive corrections and greatly assisting them in becoming published authors. Additionally, there are various other materials that require editing, such as articles, news stories, blog entries, and website content, for which owners lack the time to review. Once again, you won't even need to advertise your services.

As the gig economy continues to evolve, Fiverr has established itself as a top platform for freelancers and businesses seeking various services. Fiverr connects skilled individuals with clients in need of their expertise, covering areas such as graphic design, content creation, programming, and marketing. This in-depth guide will introduce you to Fiverr, its features, and the benefits it offers to both freelancers and businesses.

A Brief Overview of Fiverr

Fiverr, founded in 2010, is an online marketplace designed to facilitate the buying and selling of freelance services, or "gigs." With a mission to change the way the world works together, Fiverr provides a platform for freelancers to display their skills and connect with clients worldwide.

The platform's name originates from its original concept where all gigs started at $5. Although Fiverr has since expanded to include a broader range of pricing structures, its name remains synonymous with affordable and accessible freelance services.

The Functioning of Fiverr

Fiverr operates as a dual marketplace, catering to both freelancers (sellers) and clients (buyers). Here's a brief overview of how the platform functions for both parties:

For Freelancers (Sellers)

1. Create a profile: Freelancers initiate the process by creating a profile that highlights their skills, education, experience, and portfolio.

2. Set up gigs: Freelancers then establish "gigs" – individual

service offerings encompassing a description, pricing, and delivery timeline. Gigs can be tailored to offer various service tiers or add-ons at an additional cost.

3. Client communication: Once a gig is active, clients can contact the freelancer to discuss project specifics, ask questions, or place an order.

4. Project delivery: After receiving an order, the freelancer completes the project and delivers it to the client within the agreed-upon timeframe.

5. Payment and reviews: Following the project's delivery, the client can review the work, request revisions if necessary, and finalize the transaction. The freelancer receives payment, and both parties can leave feedback on their experience.

For Clients (Buyers)

1. Search for services: Clients can browse Fiverr's extensive categories or use the search function to locate freelancers offering the services they require.

2. Review freelancer profiles and gigs: Clients can examine freelancer profiles, gig descriptions, ratings, and reviews to determine the best candidate for their project.

3. Contact freelancers: Prior to placing an order, clients can communicate with freelancers to discuss project details, ask questions, or request a custom offer.

4. Place an order: Once a suitable freelancer has been found, the

client places an order, providing the necessary information and files for the project.

5. Review and approve the work: Upon receipt of the completed project, the client can review the work, request revisions if needed, and approve the final product. Payment is released to the freelancer, and both parties can leave feedback on their experience.

Advantages of Using Fiverr

Fiverr offers numerous benefits for both freelancers and businesses:

Accessibility: Fiverr presents a user-friendly platform that simplifies the process for freelancers to showcase their skills and for clients to find the services they need.

Affordability: With various pricing options available, clients can locate services that suit their budget, while freelancers can establish prices reflecting their work's value.

Diverse offerings: Fiverr features a vast array of categories and subcategories, enabling clients to find services in virtually any field and allowing freelancers to offer specialized services.

Global reach: Fiverr connects freelancers and clients from around the world, facilitating opportunities for international collaboration and access to a more extensive client base.

Fiverr is a leading freelance marketplace that provides a convenient and accessible platform for freelancers to display their skills and for clients to locate the services they require. With its wide range of categories, user-friendly interface, and global reach, Fiverr has become an indispensable resource for both freelancers and businesses in the gig economy. Whether you're a freelancer seeking to broaden your client base or a business looking for cost-effective project solutions, Fiverr is a platform worth considering.

Exploring New Skills to Enhance Your Fiverr Profile

If you find that your current skill set may not make you stand out on Fiverr, consider acquiring new skills that complement your existing ones or unlock fresh opportunities. Here are some tips for exploring new skills:

Identify gaps in the market: Look for services that are in high demand but have relatively low competition on Fiverr. Acquiring skills in these areas can help you differentiate yourself and attract clients.

Consider related skills: Ponder skills closely related to your current expertise, as they will be easier to learn and can enhance your overall service offerings.

Enroll in online courses: Numerous online platforms offer affordable courses in various subjects, enabling you to learn new skills at your own pace and convenience.

Practice, practice, practice: Developing proficiency in a new skill requires time and dedication. Commit yourself to practicing and refining your newfound skills to confidently offer them to clients.

Creating a Killer Fiverr Profile

Once you've assessed your skill set and identified new skills to acquire, it's time to create an outstanding Fiverr profile. Follow these steps to showcase your unique skills and services:

1. Choose a professional username: Ensure your username is memorable, relevant to your services, and exudes professionalism.

2. Upload a high-quality profile picture: Utilize a clear photo that presents a professional image, fostering trust and credibility among potential clients.

3. Write a compelling bio: Highlight your expertise, experience, and unique selling points concisely yet informatively in your bio. Feel free to inject some personality into your writing.

4. List your skills and expertise: Clearly outline your abilities and areas of expertise to help clients understand your offerings and why they should choose you.

5. Create detailed gig descriptions: Provide comprehensive descriptions for each gig, outlining the service, expected turnaround times, and any distinguishing features that differentiate you from competitors.

6. Incorporate relevant keywords: Research popular keywords about your services and integrate them into your profile and gig descriptions to enhance visibility in Fiverr's search results.

7. Showcase your work with samples: Display high-quality samples of your work to give clients a clear understanding of what they can expect from your services.

By following these steps, you can develop an exceptional Fiverr profile that highlights your unique skills and services, attracts potential clients, and establishes a successful presence on the platform. Remember, it takes time and dedication to build a reputation on Fiverr, so be patient and consistently deliver high-quality work to expand your client base and establish a strong presence on the platform.

Chapter Three

Starting Up Your Gig Business

S tarting your freelancing career on Fiverr is an exciting opportunity to showcase your skills and earn meaningful income. To launch your hustle successfully, you need to create a strong Fiverr account and a compelling gig that grabs attention. This chapter will guide you through these steps in a clear, beginner-friendly manner, with plenty of advice to set you on the right path.

Creating Your Fiverr Account

The first step is to sign up for Fiverr. Visit Fiverr's website or download the app, and click "Join" on the homepage to begin. You can register using your email, Google, Facebook, or Apple ID. Choose a professional and memorable username that reflects your brand or services. Since your username becomes part of your Fiverr URL, avoid choosing something unprofessional or complicated that future clients might struggle to recognize.

Next, focus on setting up an engaging and professional profile. Think of your profile as your storefront, where potential clients will learn about you and your services. Use a high-quality profile photo, either a clear and friendly picture of yourself or a logo that represents your brand. First impressions matter, so choose something polished and approachable.

Under your profile picture, add a tagline—a short statement that highlights your expertise. For example, you might say, "Creative Graphic Designer Specializing in Logos" or "Experienced Content Writer who Produces SEO-Friendly Articles." This snippet is what buyers see alongside your photo, so keep it relevant and concise.

Your profile description is the next key element. Share a bit more about your skills, experience, and what you're passionate about. This is your opportunity to make a connection with buyers. Keep your tone friendly yet professional, and focus on what makes you stand out. For instance, you could write, "I'm a digital marketer with 5 years of experience helping small businesses grow their online presence. I prioritize high-quality results and fast communication to ensure every project exceeds expectations."

Take advantage of Fiverr's options to list your skills, certifications, and languages. If you're proficient in multiple areas or have relevant credentials, display them proudly. These details help boost your credibility and attract buyers who are looking for specific qualifications. You can also link relevant social media accounts, such as LinkedIn, to further establish trust.

Planning Your First Gig

Once your account is ready, you'll want to determine what type of service you will offer in your first gig. Begin by identifying your niche. Think about what skills you have that could solve a problem or fulfill a need for potential clients.

If you're good with design, for example, you might focus on creating logos, business cards, or social media graphics. Skilled at writing? You could offer blog posts, product descriptions, or website content. Specializing in a specific area (such as "modern logo designs for startups" instead of general design work) can help you stand out in a crowded marketplace.

Spend some time browsing Fiverr to research other freelancers in your niche. Look at the gigs top-rated sellers are offering, and take notes on how they title their services, describe their offerings, and price their work. While you don't want to copy anyone directly, this research helps you understand what buyers are looking for and how you can position yourself uniquely.

When planning your gig, think about writing a clear and appealing title. Fiverr gig titles always begin with "I will," followed by the service you're offering. Aim for titles that are specific, descriptive, and include relevant keywords. For example, "I will design a creative, minimalist logo in 24 hours" is more precise than simply writing, "I will design logos."

Creating Your First Gig

Now that you've done your planning, it's time to bring your gig to life. Fiverr walks you through the process step by step, making it easy to set up. Start by crafting a title with the keywords and clarity you've already planned out. Select a category and subcategory that match your service, like "Writing & Translation" for blog writing or "Digital Marketing" for social media services. Tag your gig with related keywords to make it easier for buyers to find you.

Next, set up your pricing. Fiverr lets you create up to three service tiers—Basic, Standard, and Premium. This structure enables you to offer a range of options to suit different client budgets. For instance, if you're a writer, your Basic package could include a 500-word article, the Standard package could add SEO optimization, and the Premium option could also include multiple revisions and express turnaround. Be clear about what's included in each package so buyers understand exactly what they're getting.

The gig description plays a major role in convincing clients to choose you. Write a compelling and informative description that highlights your expertise, explains your process, and outlines the value you provide. Be specific about what's included, and don't be shy about adding a friendly touch that reflects your personality and eagerness to deliver great work. Buyers want to know they're hiring a professional who genuinely cares about their project.

Strong visuals can make your gig stand out. Upload eye-catching images, videos, or PDFs that showcase your skills. For instance, designers might add portfolio samples, writers could include writing examples or a polished PDF, and video editors might create a short reel showcasing their work. Quality visuals make a significant impression and attract clicks.

Finally, add a call to action at the end of your description, encouraging buyers to take the next step. For example, "Contact me today to discuss your project!" or "Place your order now to receive top-quality results!" makes it clear what you want potential clients to do. Review your gig details thoroughly and then hit publish. Congratulations—you're now live on Fiverr!

Setting Yourself Up for Success

Success on Fiverr doesn't come overnight, but there are steps you can take to increase your chances of landing clients quickly. Start by offering competitive pricing as a beginner to attract your first few buyers. Once you've delivered some successful projects and received a few positive reviews, you can gradually raise your rates to match your growing expertise.

Always respond to client inquiries and messages promptly. Buyers appreciate quick replies, and it shows that you're professional and dedicated. Turn on Fiverr notifications or use the mobile app to stay on top of communications wherever you are.

When you secure an order, focus on delivering exceptional results. Go above and beyond where possible, whether it's providing detailed explanations of your work process, delivering ahead of schedule, or adding small but meaningful extras. Exceptional service is what earns glowing reviews, which help your profile climb the Fiverr ranks. After completing projects, don't be afraid to politely request feedback. Reviews inspire confidence in future buyers and help you improve.

Moving Forward with Confidence

Starting on Fiverr might feel a bit overwhelming at first, but the key is to approach it step by step and stay consistent. By creating a professional profile and a carefully crafted gig, you're laying the foundation for success. Keep refining your approach based on feedback and your experiences, adapting to what works best for your services and buyers.

Remember, even top-rated sellers started with a single gig. With patience, effort, and a commitment to quality, Fiverr can become the launching pad for a successful freelancing career. Take what you've learned here, jump in, and show the world your talents!

Chapter Four

Crafting High-Quality Gigs That Sell

When it comes to selling services on Fiverr, crafting a compelling and valuable gig is the key to success. In this chapter, we'll explore three essential components of crafting high-quality gigs that sell: Developing a Unique Selling Proposition (USP), Setting Reasonable Prices for Services Rendered, and Optimizing Gig Descriptions and Images for Maximum Visibility.

Developing a Unique Selling Proposition (USP)

A Unique Selling Proposition (USP) is a feature of your business or services that sets you apart from competitors in the marketplace. It highlights what makes your offerings special and attractive to potential customers. A well-crafted USP should be both memorable and meaningful, communicating the value of your product or service in one concise statement.

When creating a USP, consider factors like cost, quality, unique features, and customer service. Additionally, think about what sets you apart from competitors—it could be specialized expertise, a wider selection of services, faster turnaround time, greater convenience, flexibility, etc.

Be sure to research the competition to identify their USPs and use them as inspiration for finding new ways to differentiate yourself. Your USP can be expressed through words or imagery such as logos and taglines; however, it's important to remember that a successful USP should convey tangible value rather than simply present an empty promise.

By employing a unique selling proposition in your gigs on Fiverr, you can spark interest among potential clients while also demonstrating your commitment to providing top-notch services. With the right message and delivery method, you can instantly stand out from the competition and make a lasting impression on customers.

To develop a strong USP, consider the following steps:

1. Identify your target audience: Understand who your ideal clients are and what they need. Consider factors such as their industry, job title, and the specific challenges they face.

2. Analyze your competition: Research other sellers offering similar products or services on the platform. Identify their strengths and weaknesses, and look for areas where you can differentiate yourself.

3. Highlight your expertise and experience: Emphasize your unique qualifications, skills, or background that make you the ideal choice for your target audience.

4. Focus on the benefits: Clearly articulate the tangible results or outcomes that clients can expect from your product or service, rather than just listing its features.

5. Keep it concise: Your USP should be a clear and concise statement that quickly communicates your value to potential clients.

Entrepreneurs often turn to Fiverr as they look for assistance in areas such as logo design, web development, marketing campaigns and more. With a wide variety of experienced professionals offering their services at competitive prices, entrepreneurs can easily find quality help without having to break the bank. Small business owners also benefit from Fiverr's array of services; from virtual assistants to administrative support, these independent contractors provide invaluable assistance at a fraction of the cost compared to hiring in-house personnel.

Content creators rely on Fiverr for tasks such as animation, video editing and other multimedia jobs. With access to experienced professionals at various price points, content creators can find the right person for their project without exceeding their budget. Students may also use Fiverr when they need help with certain assignments or projects; from ghostwriting essays and research papers to creating presentations or illustrations – there are countless talented freelancers available who could take on any task with ease.

Overall, the types of people who look for gigs on Fiverr are diverse – ranging from entrepreneurs and small business owners to content creators and students. Whether the task is large or small, there are plenty of experienced professionals ready and willing to lend a helping hand at competitive rates.

Setting Reasonable Prices for Services Rendered

Pricing your gigs appropriately is crucial for attracting clients and ensuring that you are fairly compensated for your work. When setting prices, consider the following factors:

1. Market research: Analyze the pricing strategies of competitors offering similar products or services. Use this information to establish a baseline for your own pricing structure.

2. Value-based pricing: Focus on the value you provide to clients rather than simply charging based on the time or effort required. Consider the potential return on investment (ROI) that your product or service can deliver.

3. Tiered pricing: Offer multiple pricing tiers with varying levels of service or features. This allows clients to choose the option that best fits their needs and budget.

4. Test and adjust: Monitor your sales performance over time and adjust your pricing strategy accordingly. Experiment with different price points and observe how they impact your conversion rates and overall revenue.

On Fiverr, pricing works on a tiered system. Sellers start by listing their services at the most basic level, or "Gig level" (which is $5 for most services). They can then add more features or levels of service to their Gig, allowing buyers to choose the option that best fits their needs and budget. This tier system allows sellers to charge higher prices for additional services or features - such as faster turnaround time, custom requests, and more specialized expertise - while still offering competitive pricing overall.

When setting prices on Fiverr, it's important to consider the value you are providing to clients rather than simply charging based on the time or effort required. Consider researching competitors' pricing strategies so you can set a baseline for your own pricing structure. Additionally, take into account any potential return on investment (ROI) that your product or service can provide and adjust your pricing accordingly. It's also helpful to experiment with different price points and observe how they impact your conversion rates and overall revenue.

Overall, understanding how prices work on Fiverr is essential for both attracting clients and making sure you are fairly compensated for your work. By crafting a compelling unique selling proposition (USP), setting reasonable prices for services rendered, and optimizing gig descriptions and images for maximum visibility, you can establish a successful presence on the platform while earning an income from home using your computer!

Optimizing Gig Descriptions and Images for Maximum Visibility

Gigs on Fiverr are services offered by sellers that can range from simple tasks such as writing a blog post or designing logos, to more complex projects like developing websites or creating 3D animations. Sellers create gigs that provide specific products or services to buyers for a certain fee. Fiverr offers several pricing tiers that allow sellers to charge different prices for their services depending on the complexity of the project and/or the extra features they offer.

When creating gigs, it's important to use clear, concise language that communicates the services you offer, the benefits clients can expect, and any relevant details about your process or deliverables. It's also important to incorporate relevant keywords into your gig titles and descriptions in order to increase visibility in search results. Additionally, include professional images that accurately represent your product or service and consider creating a short video to introduce yourself and explain your services.

Fiverr also allows sellers to customize their pricing structure by offering multiple tiers of service or features with varying levels of price points. This way, buyers can choose an option that best fits their needs and budget while still ensuring they get quality value at a competitive rate. Additionally, it's important for sellers to research competitors' pricing strategies so they can establish a baseline for their own gig pricing strategy based on market rates.

Overall, Fiverr provides an excellent platform for entrepreneurs looking to make money from home using their computer. By crafting compelling unique selling propositions (USPs), setting reasonable prices for services rendered, optimizing gig descriptions and images for maximum visibility, as well as monitoring sales performance over time and adjusting accordingly - sellers are presented with an opportunity to scale up their business and eventually turn it into a long-term source of income!

An effective gig description and eye-catching images are essential for attracting clients and showcasing your professionalism. To optimize your gig descriptions and images, follow these tips:

Write clear, concise descriptions: Your gig description should communicate the services you offer, the benefits clients can expect, and any relevant details about your process or deliverables. Use clear, concise language and bullet points to make your description easy to read.

Incorporate relevant keywords: Research popular keywords related to your product or service and include them in your gig title and description. This will improve your visibility in search results and help clients find your gig more easily.

Use high-quality images: Include professional, high-resolution images that showcase your work or demonstrate the outcomes clients can expect. Ensure your images are well-lit, properly composed, and accurately represent your product or service.

Add a video: Consider creating a short video to introduce yourself, explain your services, and provide a glimpse of your working process. Videos can help build trust and credibility with potential clients.

Crafting high-quality gigs that sell involves developing a strong Unique Selling Proposition, setting reasonable prices based on market research and value, and optimizing your gig descriptions and images for maximum visibility. By following these actionable strategies, you can create compelling and valuable gigs that attract clients and drive sales on platforms like Fiverr.

As you continue to hone your skills and refine your gig offerings, remember that success in the gig economy is built on persistence, adaptability, and a commitment to delivering exceptional value to your clients. Keep refining your strategies, learning from your successes and failures, and always strive to exceed your client's expectations. With dedication and a focus on quality, you'll be well on your way to thriving in the gig economy and achieving your financial goals.

Chapter Five

Managing Client Relationships Effectively on Fiverr

A s a freelancer on Fiverr, managing your client relationships is the bedrock of long-term success and steady growth. Beyond offering high-quality services, fostering strong connections with your clients can set you apart in Fiverr's competitive marketplace. Effective client management builds trust, increases repeat business, and earns you glowing reviews that attract more work. This chapter explores three key components of successful client management—establishing professional boundaries, responding promptly to inquiries, and making the most of positive reviews. By mastering these skills, you'll create a solid foundation for a thriving freelance career on Fiverr.

Establishing Professional Boundaries

Professional boundaries are essential to maintaining healthy relationships with your clients while preserving your own time, energy, and peace of mind. Without clear limits, misunderstandings and frustrations can arise, making it harder to deliver quality work. Setting boundaries isn't about being rigid or unaccommodating; it's about creating a framework that allows you to work efficiently and respectfully. Here are some strategies to help you establish and maintain those boundaries.

Communicate Expectations from the Start

The easiest way to avoid boundary issues is by being proactive. From the moment you start working with a client, make your expectations and limitations clear. For example, specify your working hours, preferred communication methods, and what's included in the scope of the services you offer.

How to communicate these boundaries effectively:

- Add your policies to your Fiverr gig descriptions. For example, include details like turnaround time, revision limits, and acceptable work hours.

- During your initial conversations, explicitly state what they can expect from you. For instance, if you don't respond to inquiries over weekends, be upfront about it.

- Confirm these specifics again when discussing project details to ensure everyone is on the same page.

For example, if a client asks you to deliver a project in 24 hours but you need 48, you might respond politely yet firmly, "I want to ensure I provide my best work, which requires at least 48 hours. Is that timeframe acceptable for you?" This approach communicates your timeline while maintaining professionalism.

Be Assertive but Professional

Even with boundaries in place, some clients might forget or overlook them. It's important to address these situations calmly and respectfully. For example, a client might send you urgent requests at midnight or request additional services beyond what was agreed.

Instead of ignoring the issue or snapping back, you can say something like, "I'd love to help, but unfortunately, I reserve late-night hours for rest to ensure I'm at my best for your project the next day. I'm happy to address this first thing tomorrow morning." You've both reaffirmed your boundary and shown your dedication to their project.

Politeness doesn't mean hesitation. Being firm serves both you and your client, ensuring a more structured and positive working relationship.

Adapt and Update Boundaries as You Evolve

Boundaries aren't static. As your freelance career evolves, so will your priorities, workflow, and availability. For instance, when you're starting out, you might accept work during unconventional hours to gain traction. Later, as your client base grows, you may choose to establish stricter limits on your availability.

Regularly assess how your current boundaries align with your goals. If they need adjustment, communicate these changes clearly and update your Fiverr gigs to reflect them. A simple message like, "To better meet the needs of all my clients, I've updated my service policies. Starting next month, I will only accept rush orders with prior approval and an extra fee," keeps your clients informed.

By establishing boundaries early, enforcing them with professionalism, and adjusting them as you grow, you pave the way for constructive and stress-free client relationships.

Responding Quickly to Client Inquiries

Responsiveness is a key factor in building trust and demonstrating your professionalism on Fiverr. Clients often favor freelancers who are prompt and attentive; it signals dependability and respect for their time. Improving your response time can set you apart in Fiverr's crowded marketplace. Below are practical ways to stay on top of inquiries and requests.

Set a Standard Response Time

Firstly, decide on a realistic response window that works for you. Whether it's a few hours during your active working time or next-day responses outside of business hours, the important thing is to be consistent and communicate that timeframe to your clients.

For example, you could include a message in your profile such as, "I typically respond to inquiries within four hours during business hours (9 AM–5 PM EST) and within 12 hours outside of these times." Giving clients clear expectations prevents frustration and ensures they feel valued.

Use Templates to Improve Efficiency

If you receive similar inquiries repeatedly, crafting thorough response templates can save you significant time. For example, if clients often ask about your availability or the need for revisions, have a personalized yet semi-automated response ready to go.

A sample template could look like this for availability inquiries: "Thank you for reaching out! I'm so excited about the possibility of working with you. I currently have availability to begin your project this week, with a standard turnaround time of [insert time]. Please feel free to share more details about your project so we can get started!"

Using templates helps you maintain a professional tone while addressing your client's needs promptly and accurately.

Leverage Technology for Timely Communication

Maximize efficiency by using tools like Fiverr's mobile app, email notifications, or integrations with project management software. Stay responsive whether you're at your desk or on the go.
For example, Fiverr's mobile app lets you respond quickly to inquiries, even if you're away from your computer. Clients appreciate prompt responses, and it prevents competitors from swooping in while they wait for you to reply.

Leveraging Positive Reviews

Reviews are the lifeblood of your reputation on Fiverr. Positive feedback from satisfied clients not only boosts your credibility but also helps you win the trust of new clients browsing for services. Here's how to make the most of them.

Encourage Reviews (Without Being Pushy)

Satisfied clients are often happy to leave reviews—they just need a little nudge. Once a project is completed, send a polite follow-up message asking for their feedback. For example, "It was a pleasure working with you! If you're happy with the final product, I would greatly appreciate it if you could leave a review on my profile. Your feedback helps me identify ways to improve and allows other clients to know they can trust my services, too. Thank you so much!"

Highlight Your Best Feedback

Don't just hope clients will see good reviews; show them off! Pin some of your most glowing reviews to your Fiverr profile or highlight them on relevant gig pages. For instance, if you specialize in creating logos, feature a review that says something like, "Amazing creativity and quick delivery—this is the best logo I've received on Fiverr!"

When potential clients see proof of your past successes, they're more likely to trust you and place an order.

Learn and Adapt from Feedback

Positive reviews are encouraging, but you can learn just as much—if not more—from constructive criticism. If a client leaves less-than-stellar feedback, take the time to reflect on what could have been done differently. Did they find your communication unclear? Were their expectations not met in terms of delivery time or quality? Use this feedback to improve and refine your approach over time.

Building a Better Future Through Client Relationships

At the core of freelancing on Fiverr is the ability to foster meaningful, professional relationships with your clients. Mastering the art of client management is about more than just ticking boxes—it's about delivering excellent service, maintaining open communication, and showing each client that they matter to you.

When you establish respectful boundaries, answer inquiries promptly, and maximize the benefits of positive reviews, you're laying the foundation for a successful, sustainable freelance career. Strong client relationships don't just bring repeat business; they enhance your reputation, open new doors, and give you a consistent edge in Fiverr's competitive marketplace.

Remember, client management is an ongoing process, not a one-time effort. By continually adapting, listening, and striving for excellence, you position yourself as a trusted professional clients can rely on. With dedication and thoughtful client care, your Fiverr freelancing career can flourish beyond your wildest expectations. Your success starts with the relationships you build—take care of those, and everything else will follow.

Chapter Six

Scaling Up and Expanding the Business

I n the previous chapters, we explored the essentials of establishing a successful business on Fiverr. Now, it's time to take your business to new heights by scaling up and expanding your operations. This chapter will delve into three key strategies for growth: diversifying your offerings, outsourcing tasks to free up time, and investing in automation tools.

Diversifying Your Offerings

To ensure long-term success, diversifying your offerings is essential. By expanding the range of services you provide, you can attract a broader client base and increase your revenue streams. Diversification also allows you to adapt to market changes and stay ahead of the competition.

Begin by conducting thorough market research. Look for emerging trends and identify in-demand services that align with your skills and expertise. Analyze your competition to understand their strengths and weaknesses and find ways to differentiate your services.

When brainstorming new service ideas, consider your target audience's needs and pain points. Engage with your existing clients to gather feedback and understand what other services they might be interested in. Testing new service ideas through small-scale experiments can help you gauge market demand before investing significant resources.

Once you've identified potential service opportunities, develop and refine your new offerings. Craft compelling service descriptions and packages that communicate the value you provide. Pricing your services appropriately is crucial to attracting clients while ensuring your efforts are adequately compensated.

Promotion and marketing play a vital role in successfully launching new services. Leverage your existing client base by announcing your new offerings and explaining how they can benefit from them. Utilize social media, email marketing, and content creation to expand your reach and attract new clients.

Outsourcing Tasks to Free Up Time

As your business grows, it becomes increasingly important to focus on your core activities. Outsourcing tasks can help you free up time and energy to concentrate on crucial aspects of your business. It also allows you to tap into the expertise of professionals in various fields, enhancing the quality of work delivered to your clients.

Identify tasks that can be effectively outsourced on Fiverr. Common examples include graphic design, copywriting, social media management, customer support, and administrative tasks. Evaluate tasks based on your own skills, time commitment, and cost-effectiveness. Consider the tasks that require specialized expertise or those that consume a significant portion of your time without directly contributing to revenue generation.

When outsourcing, clear communication is vital. Clearly define your expectations, provide comprehensive instructions, and maintain open lines of communication throughout the project. Building trust and strong relationships with the freelancers you hire will ensure smooth collaboration and satisfactory outcomes.

Fiverr provides a vast pool of talented freelancers from around the world. When searching for freelancers, carefully review their profiles, examine their portfolio, and read client reviews. Look for individuals who possess the necessary skills, have positive feedback, and align with your work style and values.

Consider starting with smaller projects to test the capabilities of potential freelancers before engaging in more significant collaborations. As you build relationships with freelancers, maintain open and effective communication channels. Establishing long-term partnerships can lead to a reliable network of freelancers who understand your business and consistently deliver high-quality work.

Investing in Automation Tools

Automation plays a vital role in streamlining processes, increasing productivity, and enabling scalability. By automating repetitive tasks, you can save time, reduce errors, and allocate your resources more efficiently. Automation also enhances the customer experience by enabling faster delivery times and consistent quality.

Evaluate your current workflows to identify tasks that can be automated on Fiverr. For instance, you can automate communication processes, order management, data entry, or even parts of your service delivery. Explore automation tools available on Fiverr's platform or external software that can integrate seamlessly with your workflow.

When considering automation, assess the feasibility and cost-effectiveness of each tool. Take into account factors such as the learning curve, setup time, and potential return on investment. Start by automating smaller tasks and gradually expand to more complex processes as you become comfortable with the technology.

Implementing automation tools requires careful planning and integration. Thoroughly understand the features and capabilities of the selected tools. Take advantage of tutorials, support resources, and community forums to familiarize yourself with the automation software.

Before fully integrating automation, test and refine the automated processes to ensure optimal functionality. Monitor the automated tasks to identify any potential issues and make necessary adjustments. Continuously evaluate the effectiveness of automation in terms of time savings, improved quality, and overall business performance.

Scaling up and expanding your Fiverr business requires strategic thinking and a willingness to embrace new opportunities. By diversifying your offerings, outsourcing tasks, and investing in automation tools, you can position your business for sustainable growth. Remember, adaptability and continuous learning are key to remaining successful in the ever-evolving world of freelancing. Take action on the strategies discussed in this chapter and keep exploring ways to enhance your business on Fiverr.

Generating Income

Undoubtedly, one of the primary motivations behind your purchase of this book is to start making money promptly. Let's crunch some numbers: if you have 20 active gigs posted on any given day, and each gig garners one order per day, you can earn a minimum of $80 in a single day.

On average, I receive about three requests per gig. If you manage to fulfill all of these requests in a day, you could potentially earn $240 in just 24 hours, which amounts to a yearly income of $87,600. While it is indeed possible to generate a full-time income from this, I won't make any grand promises. The best approach is to experience it firsthand and witness how easy it is to start making money on this platform immediately.

In the title of this book, I mentioned the figure of $800, as you can easily make $40 per day by working just five days a week. That's almost equivalent to a monthly payment on a brand-new Mercedes!

Another crucial lesson is to create a promotional video to advertise your gig. The website itself emphasizes the power of videos in marketing, although the decision is ultimately yours. I don't use videos in my gigs, and I still manage to receive an average of six requests per gig as soon as I post them. The effectiveness may vary depending on the niche, but through experimentation, you will discover your strengths and what works best for you.

Ensuring top-notch service for your customers is imperative since they can leave reviews, which greatly impacts your progression to higher levels on Fiverr. These levels are crucial as they unlock additional earning opportunities. As you advance, you can offer gig extras, such as faster delivery times, additional purchases, or upgraded quality options like high definition instead of standard definition. The potential for expanding your income is limitless.

While there are other websites similar to Fiverr, none come close to its global reach. Fiverr's reputation speaks for itself and is expected to endure for years to come. I wish you the best of luck in pursuing this opportunity. I have made several hundred dollars without spending a single dime on advertising.

Fiverr is an amazing platform for freelancers to make money and start building a successful business. With the right strategies, you can maximize your earning potential by diversifying your offerings, outsourcing tasks, investing in automation tools, creating promotional videos and providing top-notch service for customers. As long as you continue to work hard and stay up-to-date with industry trends, there's no limit on how much income you can generate from Fiverr. So why not give it a try today? The possibilities are endless!

Chapter Seven

Overcoming Challenges and Staying Motivated

B uilding a successful business as a freelancer on Fiverr is both rewarding and challenging. While the platform provides count- less opportunities to showcase your talents, navigating the inevitable hurdles can test your determination. Overcoming obstacles requires resolve, strategy, and the ability to adapt to evolving circumstances. Whether you're dealing with negative feedback, combating burnout, or learning to work smarter, addressing these issues effectively is key to long-term growth. This chapter provides practical guidance to help you tackle these challenges head-on, ensuring that you not only sur- vive but thrive in the dynamic world of freelancing.

Dealing With Negative Feedback

Negative feedback, while daunting, is a natural part of any profes- sional endeavor. Even the most seasoned freelancers face situations where a client is dissatisfied. The key lies in perceiving criticism as an opportunity to grow rather than a setback. Understanding how to handle these situations with grace will strengthen your resilience and professionalism.

Negative feedback may stem from various areas, such as unmet client expectations, miscommunication, or perceived issues with the quality of the work delivered. Sometimes, the feedback might even be a misunderstanding or an error on the client's part. Regardless, your response to criticism can make or break your professional reputation.

Responding Professionally to Feedback

When addressing negative feedback, it's critical to respond with empathy and professionalism. Begin by acknowledging the client's concerns. For example, you might say, "Thank you for your feedback—it's important to me that you're satisfied with my work." This approach immediately communicates that you value their opinion.

Position yourself as someone who is solution-oriented. If the issue was caused by unclear expectations, take steps to clarify what the client needs. For example, offer to discuss their concerns further or revise the delivery in line with their preferences. Maintain a positive demeanor and avoid defensiveness, even if the criticism feels unfair. Your ability to remain calm and cooperative will often leave a lasting impression on the client.

For instance, imagine a scenario where a client says, "The graphic design you provided isn't polished." A thoughtful response would be, "I'm sorry to hear that the design doesn't meet your expectations. Could you share specific details about what you'd like updated? I'd be happy to make revisions to ensure you're satisfied with the final product." Taking this proactive approach demonstrates your willingness to improve and highlights your commitment to quality.

Transforming Criticism Into Growth

After addressing the client's immediate concerns, take some time to reflect on the feedback with an open mind. This is not always easy, but it can reveal valuable insights. Are there patterns in client comments that suggest a recurring issue? Perhaps several clients have mentioned concerns about turnaround times, indicating an area where you could improve your workflow.

For example, if multiple clients have mentioned feeling unclear about project timelines, you could start sharing a detailed timeline at the beginning of every project. Alternatively, if the aesthetics of your designs are questioned repeatedly, consider investing time in learning new tools or trends to elevate your skill set.

Over time, you'll find that addressing constructive criticism head-on doesn't just improve your work; it bolsters your confidence as a professional. Keep in mind that even top Fiverr sellers started somewhere, and the ability to learn from feedback is what allows them to excel.

Battling Fatigue, Stress, and Burnout

Freelancing offers the freedom to craft your own work schedule, but it often comes with blurred boundaries between personal and professional life. This can lead to fatigue, stress, or even burnout, particularly during busy periods. Learning to recognize the signs of these challenges is the first step to preventing them from taking over.

Fatigue may manifest as low energy or difficulty staying focused. Stress often shows up as physical symptoms, such as headaches or difficulty sleeping, coupled with mental strain. Burnout, on the other hand, is more severe—it's a state of emotional and physical exhaustion where you may feel detached from your work.

Building Resilience Through Self-Care

Combating these challenges begins with taking care of yourself. Make sleep non-negotiable; a well-rested mind is far more productive than one operating on fumes. Incorporating regular exercise into your routine—even if it's just a quick walk—can significantly reduce stress and boost energy levels.

Learn to structure your schedule in a way that supports balance. For example, set specific working hours and communicate them to your clients. Resist the urge to check emails or start new tasks outside these hours. This simple boundary creates separation between work and down time.

Develop daily habits that recharge your mind. Meditation, journaling, or spending time in nature can be great tools to decompress. Additionally, ensuring that your workspace is organized and conducive to focus can have a surprisingly positive effect on your mental state.

Finding Motivation During Low Points

When fatigue or burnout creeps in, it's easy to lose sight of why you started freelancing in the first place. Revisit your goals and remind yourself of the bigger picture—whether it's financial independence, career growth, or the freedom to shape your own schedule. If possible, break large, overwhelming projects into smaller, more manageable tasks to regain a sense of control.

Seeking support can also make a world of difference. Reach out to fellow freelancers through social media groups or forums to share experiences and get advice. Sometimes, just knowing others face similar challenges can be reassuring.

Regularly celebrating your milestones, no matter how small, adds to your motivation. Completed your first 10 gigs? Treat yourself to something you enjoy. Achieved five-star reviews on three consecutive orders? Reflect on how far you've come. Each accomplishment can help refuel your sense of purpose.

Working Smarter, Not Harder

To grow successfully on Fiverr, you don't need to work longer hours—you need to optimize the way you work. Working smarter involves streamlining processes, utilizing tools that boost efficiency, and keeping your work methods organized.

One effective strategy is automating repetitive tasks. For instance, use email templates or automated replies to respond to frequent inquiries quickly. Tools like project management apps can also help track deadlines and client communications, ensuring nothing falls through the cracks.

Improving your workflow can also mean eliminating inefficiencies. Take a close look at your daily routine and identify areas where time is wasted. For example, if you find yourself repeatedly searching for client files, organizing them into clearly labeled folders might save you hours each week.

Batching similar tasks is another productivity goldmine. For example, dedicate one time block to brainstorming ideas for multiple clients' projects, another to responding to messages, and another to tackling revisions. This approach minimizes the mental switching costs that come from jumping between unrelated tasks.

Most importantly, as you increase your expertise, consider raising your rates rather than overloading your schedule. It's better to complete fewer, high-paying gigs to a high standard than to tackle low-paying projects that drain your time and energy.

Staying Resilient and Motivated

Freelancing on Fiverr is not a sprint—it's a marathon. Challenges like negative feedback, stress, and inefficiency are not roadblocks but opportunities to evolve. Whether overcoming a client's complaints, recalibrating your workload, or learning new tools to streamline productivity, every small improvement builds toward long-term success.

Remember, you are pursuing a career that offers freedom and opportunities unlike any other. With each obstacle you overcome, you're reinforcing your ability to thrive in this competitive yet rewarding landscape. Stay persistent, prioritize your well-being, and never stop learning. The setbacks you face today are merely steppingstones to the achievements you'll celebrate tomorrow. Keep striving, and success will undoubtedly follow.

Streamlining Processes and Automating Tasks

Automation plays a significant role in working smarter. Identify repetitive tasks that can be automated using tools and software available on Fiverr or external platforms. Automating communication processes, order management, or data entry can save time and minimize errors. Additionally, consider delegating or outsourcing tasks that can be handled by other professionals, allowing you to focus on core activities.

Leveraging Technology and Tools

Staying updated with relevant technology and tools in your field is crucial for working smarter. Research and explore software and applications that can enhance your productivity and improve the quality of your work. Project management tools, productivity apps, and collaboration platforms can streamline your workflow and facilitate effective communication with clients. Continuous learning and experimentation with new tools and techniques enable you to stay ahead of the curve and deliver exceptional results.

Overcoming challenges and staying motivated are essential for success on Fiverr. By effectively dealing with negative feedback, battling fatigue, stress, and burnout, and working smarter instead of harder, you can thrive in the competitive freelance marketplace. Embrace negative feedback as an opportunity for growth, prioritize self-care to prevent burnout, and leverage technology to optimize your workflows. Stay motivated by seeking support and finding inspiration in your journey. With resilience and determination, you can overcome challenges and achieve your goals on Fiverr.

Chapter Eight

Effective Financial Management for Fiverr Freelancers

M anaging your finances effectively is one of the most crucial aspects of building a sustainable and successful freelance business on Fiverr. While freelancing provides autonomy and flexibility, it also comes with the responsibility of handling irregular income and making wise financial decisions. Freelancers who develop strong financial management habits position themselves for long-term success and stability amidst the ups and downs of the gig economy.

This chapter focuses on two key areas of financial management that every Fiverr freelancer should prioritize—tracking income streams and budgeting wisely. Mastering these areas will provide a clear view of your earnings, empower you to make better decisions, and help you achieve your financial goals.

Tracking Income Streams

A successful Fiverr business is often built on multiple income streams, whether it's a variety of gigs, add-on services, or recurring clients.

Tracking these streams provides a detailed picture of how your business is performing, allowing you to fine-tune your efforts and focus on what generates the most value.

Understanding the Importance of Tracking Income

Keeping track of where your income is coming from is essential for making informed decisions about your work. Without this information, it's easy to overlook which gigs or clients are truly driving your business forward. For example, you may find that one service consistently brings in higher profits, while another requires more effort but yields less income. With insights like this, you can refine your focus and allocate your time more effectively.

Tracking income streams also helps you identify patterns and trends. Do certain types of gigs perform better during specific times of the year? Are new offerings gaining traction, or are tried-and-tested services still dominating your sales? Understanding these trends can guide everything from how you market your gigs to how you price your services.

Effective Methods for Tracking Your Income

Freelancers can track their income using methods tailored to their preferences and technical skills. For some, a simple spreadsheet may be sufficient, while others may benefit from advanced financial tools. The goal is to use a system that you find easy to maintain, ensuring that income tracking becomes a routine part of your financial management.

One of the most straightforward methods is creating a spreadsheet using tools like Microsoft Excel or Google Sheets. Divide columns into categories such as gig type, client name, date of order completion, and amount earned. This manual approach allows you to customize your tracking and review all the information in one place.

For freelancers who want a more efficient and automated solution, accounting software like QuickBooks or Wave can be invaluable. These platforms allow you to link your Fiverr earnings, generate income summaries, and even monitor tax-related information.

Mobile apps designed for personal finance management can also simplify tracking. Apps like Mint or PocketGuard help you categorize income, view trends, and even set financial goals. While they may not be specifically tailored to freelancers, they can still offer a bird's-eye view of your financial health.

Leveraging Your Income Data

Once you've established a consistent way to track your income, the next step is using this data to guide your decisions. Analyze the data to spot trends, identify your highest-earning services, and understand which client demographics are contributing most to your business.

For instance, you might discover that your premium website design package consistently outperforms smaller gigs in profitability. Armed with this insight, you could expand that service or invest in promoting it. Alternatively, if you notice that returning clients make up a significant portion of your revenue, you may want to focus on fostering loyalty and upselling additional services to those clients.

Understanding your Key Performance Indicators (KPIs), such as your average revenue per gig or income growth rate over time, will also provide a clear snapshot of your financial progress. Use these metrics to set goals and measure your success, ensuring your business remains on an upward trajectory.

Budgeting Wisely

While tracking income streams gives you clarity about your revenue, budgeting is what helps you take control over how that income is used. A well-crafted budget acts as a roadmap, guiding your spending and ensuring that you allocate resources where they matter most.

The Importance of Budgeting

Freelancers face unique financial challenges, such as unpredictable income and irregular expenses. Budgeting is crucial for navigating these uncertainties and maintaining financial stability. With a clear budget, you can avoid falling into the trap of overspending during good months and struggling during leaner periods.

Budgeting also ensures you're setting aside funds for essential expenses, like software subscriptions, marketing, or skill development, while safeguarding against impulsive or unnecessary spending. Over time, this discipline not only helps you control your finances but also builds a cushion for emergencies or future investments in your business.

Crafting an Effective Budget

The first step to creating a robust budget is understanding your revenue. Review your income data to project earnings over the coming months. While it's important to remain realistic, don't underestimate your potential for growth—factor in trends like seasonal demand and any plans for expanding your services.

Next, break your expenses into fixed and variable categories. Fixed expenses might include your internet service, software licenses, or Fiverr's transaction fees, while variable costs could include advertising, training courses, or purchasing materials for specific gigs. Knowing these distinctions helps you plan more efficiently.

A strong budget also includes a contingency fund. Freelancers should always expect an occasional dry spell, unexpected expense, or emergency situation. Even setting aside a small percentage of your monthly income can create a financial buffer that protects you during less predictable times.

Remember, your budget isn't just about surviving—it's about setting goals for thriving. Allocate portions of your budget toward investing in growth. For instance, you could dedicate funds to learning a new skill or upgrading your equipment to deliver even better-quality services.

Monitoring and Adapting Your Budget

Once your budget is in place, revisit it regularly. Monthly or quarterly reviews are crucial for ensuring you're staying on track. Use software or your income tracking spreadsheet to compare your budgeted expenses and income against the actual numbers. This practice will help you identify any gaps or areas where adjustments are needed.

Freelancers must also remain flexible in response to change. For example, if you've recently launched a new gig that's performing exceptionally well, you may need to increase funding for its promotion or tools. Similarly, if a service you've been offering fails to meet your profitability standards, consider reallocating resources toward a more promising venture. A budget is a living document that evolves alongside your business.

Thriving Through Financial Awareness

Mastering financial management on Fiverr takes time, but the rewards are worth it. When you actively track your income streams and use that data to refine your business strategy, you gain clarity and confidence in your decisions. Budgeting, on the other hand, helps you keep spending aligned with your long-term goals, giving you the freedom to invest in your growth without financial stress.

By building these habits into your freelancing routine, you lay the groundwork for long-term financial success. With a clear understanding of your finances, you'll be better prepared to withstand challenges, seize opportunities, and maintain control over your business's future. Managing finances might not be the most glamorous part of freelancing, but it's undoubtedly one of the most powerful tools for achieving your goals on Fiverr. Take control of your earnings, craft a budget that works for you, and empower yourself to thrive.

Chapter Nine

Long-Term Goals

L ife is filled with aspirations and dreams that inspire us to grow into our fullest potential. These long-term goals—whether they revolve around career ambitions, personal development, financial stability, or relationships—provide us with a sense of direction. They act as a compass, steering us through the uncertainties of life with the promise of something meaningful ahead. Yet, the enormity of these goals can often feel overwhelming, making the path to achieving them seem elusive. This is why breaking larger goals into smaller, manageable steps is not just helpful—it is essential. By dividing great ambitions into tangible milestones, we can transform the seemingly unachievable into a series of actionable tasks, paving the way for progress.

Recognizing the Power of Long-Term Goals

Long-term goals embody more than just ambitions—they are the visions of our desired future. They clarify what we truly want, helping us prioritize our energy and time in meaningful ways. For instance, someone aspiring to become an accomplished author envisions more than just writing a book; they dream of influencing others through their words, perhaps becoming a voice that inspires countless readers. The clearer the vision, the stronger the purpose it instills. Long-term goals also provide a framework for making decisions. When faced with daily distractions, they remind us to choose what aligns with our aspirations, ensuring we stay on course.

However, these goals can seem daunting when viewed as a single, distant endpoint. Standing at the base of what feels like a towering mountain, we might wonder how to even begin the climb. This is why the concept of breaking bigger goals into smaller steps is such a game-changer—it makes the peak appear closer and the process far less intimidating.

Making Progress Through Manageable Steps

Chunking long-term goals into manageable steps allows us to build momentum, one deliberate action at a time. Imagine wanting to switch careers and move into a new professional field. The goal it-self can feel overwhelming, especially when it involves acquiring new skills, gaining certifications, and finding industry connections. But the simple act of enrolling in an introductory course or reaching out to a mentor becomes the first rung on the ladder. Achievement builds on achievement, with each step creating a sense of accomplishment and inspiring confidence to take the next.

For example, aspiring to run a marathon might seem like a massive leap if you've never jogged a mile. Your first focus may simply be com-pleting a short walk every morning, gradually increasing the distance until you're jogging consistently. Over time, you can identify more challenging steps, such as participating in a local 5k, setting personal time goals, or following a professional training plan. Each small victory contributes to the larger dream of completing the marathon, trans-forming what once felt impossible into something within reach.

The process of breaking down goals teaches us patience and persistence. It encourages us to acknowledge that even the smallest progress carries value and that success lies in the cumulative effect of these consistent efforts.

Setting Realistic and Attainable Milestones

Milestones play a critical role in navigating the path toward any long-term goal. They act as checkpoints, providing a sense of structure and rewarding us with feelings of progress along the way. By establishing benchmarks that are both aspirational and realistic, we foster accountability and create opportunities to reflect on how far we've come. For milestones to be practical, they need to be actionable, clear, and appropriate to the stage of the journey we're currently in.

Consider the example of someone striving to save $50,000 for a down payment on their dream home. If this goal is approached without milestones, it may feel unwaveringly distant. However, setting smaller financial checkpoints, such as saving $1,000 each month, creates immediate focus. Each month's success reinforces the commitment and builds the discipline needed to achieve the ultimate objective.

Setting clear and attainable milestones also involves reflecting on the resources and support we have available. What skills need refining? What tools can we leverage? For instance, learning a new language as a long-term goal might include milestones like mastering 500 vocabulary words, completing a beginner's conversational language course, or dedicating 30 minutes each evening to practice. These smaller objectives ensure that progress is measurable while keeping your motivation intact.

Overcoming Challenges Along the Way

The road toward achieving long-term goals rarely unfolds without setbacks. Challenges—whether they come in the form of self-doubt, external obstacles, or sudden changes in circumstance—are inevitable. What defines the success of those who reach their goals is not the absence of challenges, but their ability to persevere through them. Staying motivated amidst obstacles requires self-awareness and resilience.

One common barrier is the fear of failure, which often paralyzes individuals before they even begin. Addressing that fear involves reframing failure as an opportunity to learn and grow rather than a reason to retreat. Take the example of an entrepreneur launching a small business. If the first sales campaign doesn't yield the expected results, the lessons learned about customer preferences, marketing strategies, or pricing can become valuable steppingstones toward eventual success.

Another challenge comes in the form of unexpected circumstances, whether personal or professional. Struggles such as lack of time, limited resources, or competing priorities must be met with adaptability. This often means revising smaller steps or adjusting deadlines without losing sight of the long-term goal. The practice of persistence should never be mistaken for a rigid refusal to adapt—instead, it involves staying focused while navigating life's inevitable twists.

Motivational figures can serve as guiding lights, offering inspiration while reminding us that obstacles are universal in the pursuit of significant achievements. Consider the stories of musicians who mastered their craft only after years of rejection, or athletes who returned to win championships after devastating injuries. Their experiences teach us to rely on determination and creativity to keep moving forward, even when the path seems unclear.

Continuously Evaluating and Refining Your Approach

Goal-setting is rarely a one-time activity. Progress toward long-term goals requires continuous evaluation to determine if we're moving forward effectively or drifting off course. Self-reflection provides clarity, allowing us to analyze what's working, what isn't, and what adjustments are required. Regular progress assessments can be as simple as maintaining a journal to document accomplishments and lessons learned, or as formal as quarterly reviews focused on specific metrics.

When obstacles arise or progress stalls, evaluating their underlying causes is essential. Perhaps a writer working on a novel discovers that a lack of motivation stems from unrealistic daily word count goals. By scaling back and setting more achievable targets, the writer regains focus. Similarly, an aspiring entrepreneur might realize that their marketing strategy isn't yielding the desired results. By seeking advice from mentors or learning new tactics, they refine their approach and achieve better outcomes.

Flexibility is key when revisiting strategies. Sticking rigidly to methods that don't work risks draining momentum and enthusiasm. Instead, an openness to change—whether it involves shifting priorities, altering timelines, or exploring new resources—ensures that goals remain both attainable and relevant in light of evolving circumstances.

Celebrating Milestones to Sustain Motivation

One of the most fulfilling aspects of pursuing long-term goals is recognizing and celebrating progress along the way. Acknowledging even small victories helps reinforce a positive mindset, building momentum and reaffirming your belief in your ability to succeed. Rewarding yourself at milestones bridges the gap between effort and gratification, emphasizing that each step you take has meaning.

Celebration can take many forms, depending on the goal. For someone completing the first chapter of a book, it might mean taking a day off to enjoy a favorite hobby. For someone hitting a fitness milestone, it could involve treating themselves to new workout gear. The act of celebration doesn't have to be extravagant—it simply needs to serve as a reminder that every step forward matters.

Charting a Vision for Your Future

Having experienced the value of breaking down goals and celebrating milestones, the next phase is developing a comprehensive and meaningful vision for your future. Begin by reflecting on your values, passions, and priorities. Think about what truly excites you or gives you purpose. Your long-term goals should align with these unique aspects of who you are.

Visualizing the future also involves imagining the impact achieving your goals could have—not just for yourself, but for those around you. Envision how your career aspirations might improve your family's well-being, or how personal growth could empower you to inspire others. Creating this vivid mental image fuels your determination to act and persist.

Success stems from clarity, commitment, and resilience. By setting bigger goals and tackling them through smaller steps, you gain control over your aspirations and transform dreams into reality. Each small victory adds to the foundation for greater achievements, reminding you that the destination is reached not by leaps but by strides taken one step at a time.

Chapter Ten

Bonus Material: Diversification of Income

The journey toward achieving long-term goals is rarely linear and can be filled with unexpected twists and turns. It is therefore essential to develop strategies that enable us to remain flexible, adaptable, and resilient in the face of changing circumstances. In this chapter, we will explore techniques for evaluating progress, refining our strategies, developing a plan for our future, seeking support from mentors and peers, and adapting to changing circumstances. We will also delve into bonus material on diversification of income so that we can maximize our potential for success. By equipping ourselves with these skill sets, we increase our chances of creating a fulfilling life that aligns with our passions and values.

Here are a few additional opportunities you might consider exploring further:

Freelance Writing

Possessing good writing skills can open up opportunities for free-lance writing or editing jobs on platforms like Upwork (https://www.upwork.com/), Fiverr (https://www.fiverr.com/), and Freelancer (https://www.freelancer.com/). Writing jobs span various domains, including blog posts, articles, resumes, and technical writing.

Freelance writing is an excellent way to make money from home and take control of your career. This type of work allows you to use your writing skills to create content for various online clients without having to commit to a long-term contract. You can choose when and how much you want to write, allowing you more flexibility while still earning an income.

Affiliate Marketing

Affiliate marketing involves promoting and selling products of other companies, typically through online platforms like Amazon (https://affiliate-program.amazon.com/) and eBay (https://partnernetwork.ebay.com/). As an affiliate marketer, you will receive a commission for every sale made through your referral link.

Affiliate marketing is a great way to earn passive income and build an online business. With affiliate marketing, you can generate revenue without having to physically create products yourself. This type of work requires minimal effort on your part; all you have to do is find the right product or service that resonates with your target audience and share it with them through your website or blog.

Advertising

If you have a blog or website, you can also make money from advertising. Companies are willing to pay for the privilege of displaying their advertisements on your website. The amount of money you make will depend on the traffic to your site and how click-friendly and engaging your ads are.

Advertising can be a great way to generate revenue and increase traffic to your website. You can use the extra money you make from advertising to reinvest in more content, further driving up engagement and monetization potential. Additionally, having advertisements on your website can help boost brand recognition as visitors become more familiar with the products and services being marketed.

Online Tutoring or Teaching

Websites such as Chegg Tutors (https://www.chegg.com/tutors/) , VIPKid (https://www.vipkid.com/), and Tutor.com (https://www .tutor.com/) offer opportunities to tutor students in various subjects online. Proficiency in a subject or a language can turn into a significant income source.

Online tutoring or teaching has become increasingly popular in recent years, and for good reason. With the advent of high-speed internet and advanced technology, it is now easier than ever to connect with students from all over the world and impart knowledge and wisdom in a virtual classroom.

One of the biggest advantages of online tutoring is convenience. Unlike traditional classroom settings, online tutoring allows you to work from the comfort of your own home or office. This means that you can set your own hours and work around your own schedule, making it possible to balance other commitments or pursuits.

Another advantage of online tutoring is the range of subjects that are available for tutoring. Whether you have expertise in math, science, history, language, or any other subject, there is likely a demand for your skills and knowledge. Online platforms such as Chegg Tutors, VIPKid, and Tutor.com offer a wide range of subjects and levels, so you can find the perfect match for your skills and interests.

Of course, one of the most compelling reasons to consider online tutoring is the potential income. Many online tutoring sites offer competitive rates, which can add up quickly if you're able to build up a strong client base. Depending on your qualifications and experience, you may even be able to command a higher rate and earn a significant income.

However, it's important to remember that online tutoring requires just as much dedication and professionalism as traditional in-person teaching. You will need to be prepared to create lesson plans, assign homework, and provide detailed feedback to your students. You will also need to be comfortable working with students of all ages and backgrounds, and be able to adapt your teaching style to their individual needs and learning styles.

Overall, online tutoring offers a flexible and rewarding career path for anyone with a passion for teaching and a desire to make a positive impact on students' lives. Whether you're looking to supplement your income or embark on a new career, online tutoring could be the perfect opportunity to share your knowledge and expertise with the world.

Virtual Assistance

Companies and individuals often hire virtual assistants to handle tasks like scheduling, email management, social media management, and data entry. Check out platforms like Zirtual (https://www.zirtual.com/) and Belay (https://belay.love/).

In today's fast-paced society, many businesses and individuals are looking for ways to streamline their work processes and stay organized. That's where virtual assistants come in. A virtual assistant is a remote worker who provides administrative support to clients from a remote location. Virtual assistants can handle a wide range of tasks, from basic administrative duties to more complex projects.

One of the biggest advantages of hiring a virtual assistant is cost savings. Because virtual assistants work remotely, businesses and individuals don't have to pay for office space, equipment, or benefits. This can add up to significant savings over time, especially for small businesses and entrepreneurs.

Another advantage of hiring a virtual assistant is flexibility. Virtual assistants can work from anywhere in the world, which means that they can be available to clients outside of regular business hours. This can be especially helpful for businesses that operate in different time zones, or for busy individuals who need help managing their schedules.

Virtual assistants can handle a wide range of tasks, depending on their skills and experience. Some common tasks include scheduling appointments, managing email and social media accounts, conducting research, data entry, and bookkeeping. Virtual assistants can also provide project management support, such as coordinating events and preparing presentations.

If you're interested in hiring a virtual assistant, there are a number of platforms and services that can help. Zirtual and Belay are two popular options. These platforms provide access to a pool of qualified virtual assistants, so you can find the perfect match for your needs. Once you've found a virtual assistant that you like, you can communicate with them remotely and set up a work schedule that works for both of you.

Overall, virtual assistants offer a flexible and cost-effective way to manage administrative tasks and stay organized. Whether you're a small business owner, an entrepreneur, or just someone who needs help managing their day-to-day tasks, a virtual assistant could be the perfect solution.

Transcription Services

Websites like Rev (https://www.rev.com/) and TranscribeMe (https://www.transcribeme.com/) hire people to transcribe audio files. If you have fast and accurate typing skills, this could be a good fit.

Transcription services have become increasingly popular in recent years, and for good reason. Businesses and individuals alike need accurate and efficient transcriptions of audio files for a variety of purposes, from legal proceedings to market research interviews. Fortunately, there are now a number of online platforms that offer transcription services, making it easier than ever to find the help you need.

One of the most popular platforms is Rev. Rev offers a wide range of transcription services, from audio and video transcription to closed captioning and subtitling. With over 50,000 freelancers around the world, Rev is able to offer quick turnaround times and high-quality transcriptions at competitive rates.

Another popular platform is TranscribeMe. TranscribeMe specializes in fast, accurate transcriptions using state-of-the-art technology and a large network of experienced transcribers. The platform also offers customizable transcription solutions to meet the specific needs of businesses and organizations.

If you have fast and accurate typing skills, transcription services could be a good fit for you. Many transcription platforms, including Rev and TranscribeMe, hire remote workers to transcribe audio files from home. This means that you can work on your own schedule and earn money from anywhere in the world.

However, it's important to note that transcription can be a challenging and time-consuming task. Transcribers must have excellent listening skills and be able to type quickly and accurately while maintaining focus for long periods of time. Additionally, some audio files may contain difficult accents or technical jargon, which can make transcription even more challenging.

Overall, transcription services offer a valuable solution for businesses and individuals who need accurate and efficient transcriptions of audio files. Whether you're a remote worker looking for flexible job opportunities or a business owner in need of transcription services, platforms like Rev and TranscribeMe can help you get the job done.

Online Surveys or Market Research

Websites like Swagbucks (https://www.swagbucks.com/), Vindale Research (https://www.vindale.com/), and MTurk (https://www.mturk.com/) offer payment for taking surveys, participating in market research, or performing simple online tasks.

Online surveys and market research have become increasingly popular as businesses seek to gather insights from consumers about their products and services. This has created an opportunity for individuals to earn money by participating in online surveys and market research studies. There are a number of websites that offer payment for these activities, including Swagbucks, Vindale Research, and MTurk.

Swagbucks is one of the most popular platforms for online surveys and market research. The platform offers a wide range of surveys on various topics, as well as other opportunities to earn money, such as watching videos and shopping online. Swagbucks pays users in points, which can be redeemed for gift cards or cash via PayPal.

Vindale Research is another popular platform that offers payment for online surveys and market research. Users can earn up to $50 per survey, as well as additional bonuses for referring friends to the platform. Vindale Research also offers users the opportunity to participate in product testing and focus groups for even higher payouts.

MTurk, or Amazon Mechanical Turk, is a platform that allows users to perform simple online tasks for payment. These tasks can include data entry, transcription, and image tagging, among others. While the payouts for individual tasks may be relatively small, users can earn a significant amount over time by completing a large volume of tasks.

While participating in online surveys and market research can be a great way to earn extra income, it's important to be aware of potential pitfalls. Some websites may not be legitimate and could be scams, while others may not pay as much as they claim. It's important to do thorough research before signing up for any survey or market research website, and to read reviews and feedback from other users.

Overall, online surveys and market research offer a convenient and flexible way to earn money from home. Whether you're looking for a side hustle or a full-time gig, websites like Swagbucks, Vindale Research, and MTurk can help you earn money while sharing your opinions and insights with businesses and organizations.

Website or App Testing

Platforms like UserTesting (https://www.usertesting.com/) pay users to test websites and apps and provide feedback.

Website and app testing has become an essential part of the development process for many companies. By soliciting feedback from users, businesses can identify and fix issues before launching their products to the public. Fortunately, there are now a number of platforms that offer payment for website and app testing, making it possible for individuals to earn money by providing valuable feedback.

One of the most popular platforms for website and app testing is UserTesting. UserTesting offers a range of testing services, including website testing, mobile app testing, and prototype testing. Users are paid to complete tasks on websites or apps while providing feedback on their user experience. UserTesting pays its testers $10 per 20-minute test, which can add up quickly for frequent testers.

Another popular platform is TryMyUI. TryMyUI offers website and app testing services to businesses and organizations, using a network of remote testers around the world. Testers are paid to provide feedback on their user experience, as well as suggestions for improvement. TryMyUI pays its testers $10 per test, with each test taking approximately 20 minutes to complete.

If you're interested in website or app testing, it's important to note that you don't need any special skills or qualifications to get started. However, you should have strong attention to detail and be able to provide clear and concise feedback. It's also important to have access to a computer and a reliable internet connection, as most testing is done online.

Overall, website and app testing can be a great way to earn extra income while providing valuable feedback to businesses and organizations. Whether you're a tech enthusiast or just someone looking for a flexible side hustle, platforms like UserTesting and TryMyUI can help you get started.

E-commerce

Selling products online through platforms like Etsy (https://www.et sy.com/) for handmade or vintage items, eBay (https://www.ebay.co m/), or Amazon (https://www.amazon.com/) can be quite profitable. You might also consider dropshipping, which involves selling products that are fulfilled by a third party.

E-commerce has become a popular way for individuals to make money online. With the rise of online marketplaces like Etsy, eBay, and Amazon, it's easier than ever to sell products to customers around the world. Here are some tips for making money through e-commerce.

One of the easiest ways to get started is by selling handmade or vintage items on Etsy. Etsy provides a platform for individual sellers to showcase their unique products, reaching a global audience of buyers. Whether you're a skilled artist, crafter, or collector, there's likely a market for your products on Etsy.

Another popular platform for e-commerce is eBay. eBay is an online marketplace where users can buy and sell just about anything, from electronics to clothing to collectibles. eBay offers a range of features to help sellers promote their products and connect with potential buyers, including auctions, buy-it-now options, and advertising tools.

Of course, one of the biggest players in the e-commerce space is Amazon. Amazon offers a range of services for sellers, from basic product listings to advanced fulfillment options through Amazon FBA (Fulfillment by Amazon). With over 300 million active customers worldwide, Amazon can provide a huge audience for sellers looking to expand their reach.

Another increasingly popular option is dropshipping. Dropshipping involves selling products that are fulfilled by a third party, such as a manufacturer or wholesaler. This allows sellers to offer a wide range of products without having to store inventory or handle shipping themselves. Dropshipping can be a great way to get started in e-commerce with relatively low startup costs.

Overall, e-commerce offers a wealth of opportunities for individuals looking to make money online. Whether you're interested in selling handmade goods, vintage items, or other products, platforms like Etsy, eBay, and Amazon can provide the tools and audience you need to succeed. Alternatively, dropshipping can be a great way to offer a wide range of products without the hassle of managing inventory and shipping.

Stock Photography

If you're adept at photography, you can sell your photos online through platforms like Shutterstock (https://www.shutterstock.com/) or iStock (https://www.istockphoto.com/).

Stock photography is a popular way for photographers to earn money online by selling their images through various stock photography platforms. If you have a keen eye for photography, this could be an excellent opportunity to monetize your skills and potentially make a significant amount of money.

Shutterstock and iStock are two of the most popular stock photography platforms that allow photographers to sell their images to clients who need stock photos for various purposes such as marketing, advertising, or website design. These platforms offer photographers an opportunity to showcase their work to a global audience and earn money in the process.

One of the biggest advantages of selling stock photos is that it can be a passive income stream. Once your photos are uploaded to the platform, they can be downloaded and purchased by clients repeatedly over time. This means that you can continue to earn money from the same images long after you've taken them.

However, it's important to note that competition in the stock photography industry can be fierce. With so many photographers vying for attention, it's important to create high-quality images that stand out from the crowd. You'll also need to be aware of copyright laws and ensure that you have the necessary rights to sell the images you upload.

If you're interested in selling stock photos online, there are a number of tips that can help you succeed. First, focus on creating images that are marketable and in-demand. This might involve researching current trends and popular themes in the industry. Second, ensure that your photos are of high quality and meet the technical requirements of each platform. Finally, be prepared to market your photos and promote your work through social media and other channels to attract potential clients.

Overall, stock photography can be a profitable and enjoyable way to monetize your photography skills. Whether you're a professional photographer looking to supplement your income or an amateur photographer hoping to turn your hobby into a side hustle, platforms like Shutterstock and iStock can provide the tools and audience you need to succeed.

Affiliate Marketing

Running a blog or maintaining a robust social media presence can be monetized through affiliate marketing. This involves promoting a product and earning a commission on any sales made through your link.

Affiliate marketing is a popular way for individuals to make money online through promoting products and earning commissions on any resulting sales. If you have a blog or a strong social media presence, affiliate marketing can be an excellent opportunity to monetize your platform and potentially earn a significant amount of money.

Affiliate marketing involves partnering with companies that offer products or services relevant to your audience. As an affiliate, you'll promote these products through various channels, such as your blog or social media accounts, and include a special link that directs users to the company's website. If a user clicks on your link and makes a purchase, you'll earn a commission on the sale.

One of the biggest advantages of affiliate marketing is its flexibility. You can choose which products to promote and how to promote them, giving you control over the content you create and the messages you convey to your audience. Additionally, affiliate marketing can be a passive income stream, allowing you to earn money from your existing content long after it has been published.

To get started with affiliate marketing, you'll first need to identify companies and products that are a good fit for your audience. Consider factors such as your niche, your target demographic, and your existing content when choosing which companies to partner with. Once you've identified potential partners, you can sign up for their affiliate programs and start promoting their products through your blog or social media channels.

It's important to note that succeeding in affiliate marketing requires more than simply including links in your content. To truly succeed, you'll need to create high-quality content that resonates with your audience and effectively promotes the products you're affiliated with. This might involve creating product reviews, tutorials, or other types of content that provide value to your readers while also promoting the products you're affiliated with.

Overall, affiliate marketing offers a flexible and potentially lucrative way to make money online. Whether you're a blogger, influencer, or social media personality, affiliate marketing can provide the tools and opportunities you need to monetize your platform and earn money through promoting products and services.

Online Content Creation

If you have a unique skill or hobby, creating content for a blog, YouTube (https://www.youtube.com/), a podcast, or a paid newsletter can bring income.

Online content creation has become a popular way for individuals to monetize their skills and hobbies by creating content that appeals to a wide audience. Whether you're a writer, artist, musician, or simply someone with a unique perspective on the world, creating online content can be an excellent way to turn your passion into a profitable venture.

There are numerous platforms available for creating online content, including blogs, YouTube, podcasts, and paid newsletters. Each platform offers its own unique advantages and challenges, so it's important to choose the one that best suits your skills and interests.

Blogging is one of the most popular platforms for online content creation. With a blog, you can write about virtually any topic that interests you and share your thoughts and insights with a global audience. Blogging can be particularly effective for niche topics, as it allows you to connect with readers who share your interests and passions.

YouTube is another popular platform for content creators. With over 2 billion monthly active users, YouTube offers a huge audience for individuals looking to create video content. Whether you're a comedian, musician, or tutorial creator, there's likely an audience for your content on YouTube.

Podcasting has also become a popular platform for content creators, particularly those with a talent for storytelling or conversation. With a podcast, you can create audio content that engages listeners and provides valuable information or entertainment. Podcasts can be particularly effective for building a loyal audience and establishing yourself as an authority in your niche.

Finally, paid newsletters are a relatively new platform for online content creation. With a paid newsletter, you can provide exclusive content to subscribers who are willing to pay for access. This can be an effective way to monetize your expertise and provide value to readers who are interested in your unique perspective on the world.

Overall, online content creation offers a wealth of opportunities for individuals looking to monetize their skills and interests. Whether you're a writer, artist, musician, or simply someone with a unique perspective on the world, there's likely a platform that can help you reach a global audience and earn a significant amount of money in the process.

Freelance Graphic Design

Skilled graphic designers can offer their services to clients on platforms like Fiverr (https://www.fiverr.com/), Upwork (https://www.upwork.com/), and 99designs (https://99designs.com/).

Freelance graphic design has become a popular way for skilled designers to make money online by offering their services to clients around the world. With the rise of online platforms like Fiverr, Upwork, and 99designs, it's easier than ever for graphic designers to connect with clients and build a thriving freelancing business.

Fiverr is one of the most popular platforms for freelance graphic design. With Fiverr, designers can create a profile and offer their services to clients around the world. Fiverr offers a wide range of features to help designers promote their work and connect with potential clients, including a messaging system, portfolio showcase, and advertising tools. Payments are made through the platform, and Fiverr takes a small commission on each transaction.

Upwork is another popular platform for freelance graphic design. Upwork allows designers to bid on projects posted by clients, creating a competitive marketplace for design services. Upwork offers a range of tools to help designers manage their workflow, including time tracking, invoicing, and project management tools. Payments are made through the platform, and Upwork takes a commission on each transaction.

Finally, 99designs is a platform that focuses specifically on graphic design services. With 99designs, clients can post design projects and receive submissions from a pool of talented designers. Clients can then choose their favorite design and work with the designer directly to refine the final product. 99designs pays designers directly for their work, with no commissions taken.

To succeed as a freelance graphic designer, it's important to have a strong portfolio of work that showcases your skills and expertise. You should also be able to communicate effectively with clients and be able to manage your workflow efficiently. Additionally, you'll need to be familiar with industry-standard design software, such as Adobe Photoshop and Illustrator, and stay up-to-date on current design trends and techniques.

Overall, freelance graphic design can be a rewarding and financially lucrative way to make money online. Whether you're a seasoned designer looking to build your own business, or a beginner looking to get started in the industry, online platforms like Fiverr, Upwork, and 99designs can provide the tools and opportunities you need to succeed.

It's important to thoroughly research each opportunity and remain vigilant against potential scams. Earning $800 per month might take some time to achieve, but with persistence and consistency, it's attainable.

Chapter Eleven

Bonus #2: Free Web Resources to Make Even More!

T he online economy has exploded in recent years, and there are now countless opportunities to make extra income, ranging from doing small tasks or gigs to selling goods or services, participating in market research, or even sharing your skills and knowledge.

Please note, always do your own research before signing up for a platform to ensure that it's reputable and fits your needs. Here are 100 websites where you might be able to make some extra money:

1. Upwork - www.upwork.com

2. Fiverr - www.fiverr.com

3. Freelancer - www.freelancer.com

4. Etsy - www.etsy.com

5. Amazon Mechanical Turk - www.mturk.com

6. UserTesting - www.usertesting.com

7. Swagbucks - www.swagbucks.com

8. Clickworker - www.clickworker.com

9. Airbnb - www.airbnb.com

10. Uber - www.uber.com

11. Lyft - www.lyft.com

12. TaskRabbit - www.taskrabbit.com

13. Turo - www.turo.com

14. Rover - www.rover.com

15. JustAnswer - www.justanswer.com

16. Shutterstock - www.shutterstock.com

17. Poshmark - www.poshmark.com

18. eBay - www.ebay.com

19. Toptal - www.toptal.com

20. Skillshare - www.skillshare.com

21. Survey Junkie - www.surveyjunkie.com

22. Teachable - www.teachable.com

23. 99Designs - www.99designs.com

24. Redbubble - www.redbubble.com

25. Postmates - www.postmates.com

26. DoorDash - www.doordash.com

27. Instacart - www.instacart.com

28. Chegg Tutors - www.chegg.com/tutors

29. VIPKID - www.vipkid.com

30. Zirtual - www.zirtual.com

31. FlexJobs - www.flexjobs.com

32. ThredUP - www.thredup.com

33. Udemy - www.udemy.com

34. Rev - www.rev.com

35. InboxDollars - www.inboxdollars.com

36. Guru - www.guru.com

37. Cafepress - www.cafepress.com

38. Dribbble - www.dribbble.com

39. Patreon - www.patreon.com

40. GoFundMe - www.gofundme.com

41. Kickstarter - www.kickstarter.com

42. Indiegogo - www.indiegogo.com

43. Cambly - www.cambly.com

44. Decluttr - www.decluttr.com

45. Gazelle - www.gazelle.com

46. SellCell - www.sellcell.com

47. UserZoom - www.userzoom.com

48. Respondent - www.respondent.io

49. Ecomhunt - www.ecomhunt.com

50. ProZ - www.proz.com

51. Designhill - www.designhill.com

52. Behance - www.behance.net

53. Voices.com - www.voices.com

54. Userlytics - www.userlytics.com

55. Pinecone Research - www.pineconeresearch.com

56. Zazzle - www.zazzle.com

57. Teespring - www.teespring.com

58. CafePress - www.cafepress.com

59. Bonanza - www.bonanza.com

60. Society6 - www.society6.com

61. BookScouter - www.bookscouter.com

62. CardPool - www.cardpool.com

63. Sittercity - www.sittercity.com

64. Care.com - www.care.com

65. Qkids - www.qkids.com

66. Textbroker - www.textbroker.com

67. iWriter - www.iwriter.com

68. Constant Content - www.constant-content.com

69. HireWriters - www.hirewriters.com

70. Scribendi - www.scribendi.com

71. EditFast - www.editfast.com

72. Squadhelp - www.squadhelp.com

73. NamingForce - www.namingforce.com

74. UserFeel - www.userfeel.com

75. Loop11 - www.loop11.com

76. TryMyUI - www.trymyui.com

77. Userbrain - www.userbrain.net

78. TestingTime - www.testingtime.com

79. Babbletype - www.babbletype.com

80. Sigtrack - www.sigtrack.net

81. ClickNwork - www.clicknwork.com

82. Humanatic - www.humanatic.com

83. Qmee - www.qmee.com

84. Prolific - www.prolific.co

85. PrizeRebel - www.prizerebel.com

86. GrabPoints - www.grabpoints.com

87. Dosh - www.dosh.com

88. Rakuten - www.rakuten.com

89. Paribus - www.paribus.co

90. MyPoints - www.mypoints.com

91. Shopkick - www.shopkick.com

92. CheckPoints - www.checkpoints.com

93. Field Agent - www.fieldagent.net

94. Gigwalk - www.gigwalk.com

95. EasyShift - www.easyshiftapp.com

96. Fotolia - www.fotolia.com

97. iStockPhoto - www.istockphoto.com

98. Dreamstime - www.dreamstime.com

99. Alamy - www.alamy.com

100. 123RF - www.123rf.com

The opportunities are truly endless when it comes to making money online. Good luck with your ventures!

About the Author

Gerry Marrs is a distinguished author renowned for his deep passion for aviation and flying, seamlessly blending his expertise in research, data science, and artistry into his captivating narratives. Beyond his professional achievements, Gerry is a devoted spouse and loving parent to four affectionate dogs, embodying warmth and dedication in both his personal and public life. With a talent that has earned him global acclaim, Gerry continues to inspire and uplift many, showcasing the impact of pursuing one's passions and sharing one's gifts with the world.

Also by Gerry Marrs Publicatons

How to Make Money Writing Product Reviews: Make Extra Money Getting Free Products Sent to Your Door

https://www.amazon.com/dp/B00LDUGED8

Discover the secret to transforming your writing skills into a lucrative venture with "How to Make Money Writing Product Reviews: Make Extra Money Getting Free Products Sent to Your Door". This comprehensive guide offers you the golden opportunity to earn extra income from home by providing valuable feedback on new products, all while receiving them for free. Dive into the world of product reviews, where your opinion not only matters but also pays. With expert strategies and actionable advice, this book teaches you how to create engaging, sales-driving reviews, secure free products, find high-paying clients, and effectively manage your time to maximize your earnings. Whether you're looking to make some extra cash on the side or establish a full-fledged business, this guide equips you with everything you need to succeed in the booming market of product reviews. Start your journey towards financial freedom today by unlocking the potential of your pen with this indispensable resource.

Free Money For Nearly Anything: Start a Business, Buy a New Home, Free Benefits for Veterans

https://www.amazon.com/dp/B00UCNHBMA

Prepare to be astounded as you uncover the secrets of effortlessly accessing funds you never knew you could claim with "Free Money For Nearly Anything: Start a Business, Buy a New Home, Free Benefits for Veterans". This isn't just wishful thinking; it's your guide to tapping into a wealth of resources available to those savvy enough to seek them. Whether it's kickstarting your dream venture, purchasing your ideal home without the burden of loans, unlocking exclusive benefits for veterans, or securing scholarships that make education affordable, this book is a treasure map to financial aid that doesn't require repayment. It demolishes the myth of "too good to be true" with solid, proven strategies that have already changed lives. Beyond mere financial gain, it's about the freedom and opportunities that come with it. As the saying goes, the early bird catches the worm, and with this book, you're on the verge of discovering a sunrise of possibilities. Don't let skepticism hold you back from learning the ins and outs of acquiring free money. This book isn't just a revelation; it's a revolution in managing your finances and achieving your dreams. The clock is ticking, and it's time to start your treasure hunt. Grab your copy now and step into a world where financial freedom is not just a dream, but a reality waiting to be claimed.

How to Legally Rob Credit-Card Companies: Get Out of Debt Faster, Raise Your Credit Score, and Finally Live Free!

https://www.amazon.com/dp/B00HLJIVWM

Step into a realm of financial empowerment with "How to Legally Rob Credit-Card Companies: Get Out of Debt Faster, Raise Your Credit Score, and Finally Live Free!". This isn't merely a book; it's a lifeline thrown to those drowning in debt, battling high interest rates, and suffering from poor credit scores. It offers a fresh start, a path to financial liberation that beckons you to shed the chains of fiscal constraints. With the latest strategies and insights, this guide provides a clear roadmap through the ever-changing landscape of finance, equipping you with the tools to navigate debt, enhance your credit score, and reclaim your financial autonomy. By demystifying complex concepts and introducing proven techniques for debt management and financial growth, this book is a beacon of hope for anyone yearning to take control of their economic destiny. Alongside, it offers an exclusive treasure trove of resources, from cutting-edge financial tools to links and directories that support your journey to a debt-free life. Whether you're aiming to improve your financial literacy, manage your debts more effectively, or explore income-boosting and investment strategies, this guide is your comprehensive resource for building a robust, prosperous future. Embark on your journey toward financial freedom today by embracing the transformative wisdom within these pages. Your financial revolution begins now.

How to Make $800 Per Month Starting Tonight!: A "no-hype" realistic plan you can implement immediately, without spending a dime of your own!

https://www.amazon.com/dp/B00HLW5GFE

Dive into the heart of financial liberation with "Make $800 Per Month Starting Tonight!" – your definitive guide to conquering the gig economy, crafted by the visionary Gerry Marrs. This transformative book isn't just a read; it's a radical shift towards achieving the financial freedom you've always aspired to. It reveals the untapped potential within you and the digital marketplace, guiding you to leverage your skills in a world where technology paves the way to unprecedented earnings. From crafting captivating gigs that sell themselves on platforms like Fiverr to mastering the art of passive income through skillful diversification, this book is a comprehensive blueprint for success. It teaches you not only to earn but to multiply your earnings by automating, outsourcing, and tapping into a myriad of income streams. Whether you're looking to make a significant side income or transform your financial landscape entirely, Gerry Marrs delivers the wisdom, strategies, and actionable steps to make it a reality. "Make $800 Per Month Starting Tonight!" is not just a promise; it's a proven pathway to financial success and autonomy in the gig economy. The future of work is here, and with this book, you're poised to claim your piece of the pie. Are you ready to embrace your financial freedom, the Gerry Marrs way? The journey to a more prosperous life begins tonight.

How to Become a Profitable Money Broker: Make $100,000 per year assisting clients in finding low interest rate loans to start a business, buy a new home, or make major, life-changing purchases

https://www.amazon.com/dp/B01M0MJKXI

Dive into the lucrative world of money brokering with "How to Become a Profitable Money Broker" and discover the pathway to a potential $100,000 per year income by connecting clients with low-interest loans for business startups, home purchases, or pivotal life events. This comprehensive guide is your blueprint to mastering the ins and outs of the money broker industry, offering deep insights into the demand for financial services and the skills needed to succeed. From understanding the nuances of mortgage, business, and personal loans to developing key negotiation and financial literacy skills, this book equips you with everything required to build a thriving broker-age. Learn how to set up your business, attract clients, navigate the loan application process, and negotiate favorable terms, all while managing and scaling your enterprise for long-term success. With bonus content including secret websites for income diversification, this book is an invaluable resource for anyone looking to make a significant impact in the financial services sector and achieve financial freedom.

----

60 Days to $60,000: Building a Home Business with Practically Zero Startup Costs

https://www.amazon.com/dp/B01M1FXIJ9

Step into a world where financial freedom is not just a dream, but a well-charted course with the revised and enhanced edition of "60 Days to $60,000: Building a Home Business with Practically Zero Startup Costs". This edition isn't merely an update; it's a comprehensive over-haul designed to catapult you towards your goal of earning $60,000 in just two months, from the comfort of your home. With a focus on practicality, this guide dismantles the myths surrounding home businesses, laying out a clear, actionable plan for success with minimal financial outlay. It teaches you how to leverage the power of organic growth through strategies like email marketing and storytelling, without the need for expensive advertising. The expanded bonus section offers an arsenal of tools, templates, and techniques to streamline your operations, while new chapters on community building and strategic partnerships highlight the importance of networking in today's entrepreneurial landscape. Whether you're a budding entrepreneur or an established businessperson looking for fresh insights, "60 Days to $60,000" promises not just a method but a transformation, turning ambitious visions into tangible successes.

How to Achieve Anything You Want: Set and Prioritize Goals, Attract Wealth, Live the Life You Always Dreamed

https://www.amazon.com/dp/B00KEHI65K

Unlock the blueprint to an extraordinary life with "How to Achieve Anything You Want: Set and Prioritize Goals, Attract Wealth, Live the Life You Always Dreamed." This transformative guide empowers you to break free from mediocrity by setting clear, actionable goals and harnessing the power of visualization to manifest your dreams into reality. Dive deep into strategies that will help you overcome obstacles, rewire limiting beliefs, and cultivate a mindset of success and abundance. Learn how to design a personalized roadmap to achieve your dreams while maintaining a balanced, fulfilling life. Whether it's financial prosperity, career achievements, or personal well-being you seek, this book offers the tools and insights to attract wealth and happiness. Embrace the journey towards living the life you've always desired, equipped with the knowledge and tactics to unleash your potential and achieve anything you set your mind to.

How to Get Rich with Other People's Stuff: Make up to $5,000 per Month With Products You Don't Even Own!

https://www.amazon.com/dp/B00SP6ME82

Dive into the world of entrepreneurial success with "How to Get Rich with Other People's Stuff" and unlock the door to earning up to $5,000 per month without owning a single product. This innovative guide offers a fresh perspective on wealth creation, revealing how to capitalize on leveraging others' products to establish a lucrative home-based business with minimal startup costs. Perfect for both seasoned entrepreneurs and those new to the business world, this book provides a step-by-step blueprint for building a flexible, profitable venture that allows you to control your time and income. Discover unique business models, multiple income avenues, and passive income strategies that enable you to earn effortlessly, without the hard sell. Packed with real-life success stories and actionable advice, this book is your key to escaping financial limitations and embracing a future of abundance. Start your journey toward financial freedom today and transform your entrepreneurial dreams into reality with the groundbreaking strategies found within these pages.

Quit Smoking in Nine Days: Breathe Easier, Restore Your Health, Live Longer!

https://www.amazon.com/dp/B00QLFKR4C

Embark on a transformative journey with "Quit Smoking in Nine Days: Breathe Easier, Restore Your Health, Live Longer!" by Gerry Marrs, a comprehensive guide designed to free you from the clutches of smoking in under two weeks. This book is more than just a series of steps; it's a holistic approach to quitting smoking that covers everything from nutrition and exercise to stress management, ensuring your path to quitting is not only successful but also enhances your overall well-being. With practical, day-by-day instructions, Marrs simplifies the quitting process, making a smoke-free life an achievable goal. Additionally, the book provides insights into building a supportive network, managing withdrawal symptoms, and staying motivated with inspiring success stories and motivational strategies. It also includes exclusive access to bonus resources like helpful apps and communities, making it a robust toolkit for anyone ready to quit smoking and embrace a healthier, longer life. "Quit Smoking in Nine Days" stands out for its focus on nourishment, holistic health, and the emphasis on longevity, offering readers a compelling vision of their smoke-free future.

How to Burn Fat and Lose Weight Ridiculously Easy: Even During the Holidays!

https://www.amazon.com/dp/B00GVHWMMU

Discover the joy and simplicity of shedding pounds without sacrificing the festive spirit with "How to Burn Fat and Lose Weight Ridiculously Easy: Even During the Holidays!" This groundbreaking guide overturns traditional weight loss dogmas, presenting a surprisingly simple, yet effective strategy for burning fat: walking. By embracing a gentle, consistent walking routine, you'll unlock your body's natural fat-burning capabilities, enabling you to indulge in holiday cheer without the fear of weight gain. This book doesn't just offer exercise advice; it's a holistic approach to well-being, incorporating stress reduction techniques and heart rate monitoring to optimize your health journey. Whether navigating the temptations of Thanksgiving, Christmas, or any festive occasion, you'll learn how to enjoy your favorite treats guilt-free. With practical tips on maintaining a balanced lifestyle amidst the hustle and bustle of holiday seasons, this book ensures your weight loss journey is not only effective but also stress-free and enjoyable. Start walking your way to a slimmer, healthier you, and experience the power of a rejuvenated body and mind, no matter the time of year.

www.ingramcontent.com/pod-product-compliance
Lightning Source LLC
Chambersburg PA
CBHW030901180526
45163CB00004B/1657